Evangelical Heathenism?

Examining Contemporary Revivalism

E. Calvin Beisner

Canon Press

MOSCOW, IDAHO

E. Calvin Beisner, *Evangelical Heathenism? Examining Contemporary Revivalism*

 Published by Canon Press, P.O. Box 8741, Moscow, ID 83843

99 98 97 96 9 8 7 6 5 4 3 2 1

Cover design by Paige Atwood Design, Moscow, ID.

Printed in the United States of America.

ISBN: 1-885767-18-8

To Arthur John:

Sanctify the Lord Christ in your heart, always being ready to make a defense to everyone who asks you to give an account for the hope that is in you, yet with gentleness and reverence; and keep a good conscience so that in the thing in which you are slandered, those who revile your good behavior in Christ may be put to shame.

1 Peter 3:15-16

Table of Contents

Acknowledgments

First and foremost, my thanks go to Dr. Alan W. Gomes, professor of theology at Talbot Theological Seminary, my dear friend and fellow laborer in the defense of the gospel, for his teamwork through over fifteen years in research and writing on this subject. A fearless defender of the faith once delivered to the saints, he has long been on the front line of battle, often alone as a visible target for opponents, in the ongoing debate of which this publication is a part. May God richly reward you, Alan, for the sacrificial service you have rendered in this cause.

Second, thanks to Doug Jones and Canon Press for their willingness to publish this book. Their labors not only in defense of the gospel but also in the broader work of the Kingdom of God are to be commended.

Third, thanks to Dr. Jay Grimstead, director of The Coalition on Revival, and to the members of COR's Theological Review Committee, Dr. Gleason Archer of Trinity Evangelical Divinity School, Dr. Henry Krabbendam of Covenant College, Dr. Harold Lindsell, Dr. Larry Walker of Mid-America Baptist Theological Seminary, Dr. Michael Rusten, and Victor Porlier who cooperated several years ago in my preparing for the committee a critique of Moral Government Theology that was one step along the road to this book and is reprinted here, with minor adaptations, as Chapter 3.

E. Calvin Beisner
Chattanooga, Tennessee
September 4, 1996

Soli Deo Gloria!

Introduction

Judy's Story

Judy had been on the mission field for nearly ten years with a group of vibrant young people. She had served in Switzerland in a variety of ways and then had accepted a position in Brother Andrew's ministry, God's Open Doors. Hers had been a steady, consistent walk. She should have been filled with the joy and satisfaction of faithful service in the Kingdom of God.

But when she came to the Christian Research Institute in 1976, Judy was depressed to the point of despair. In the last three years, her once vibrant, joyful relationship with God had become dry and joyless. She wondered out loud not whether she would be able to regain the joy her faith had once given her, not even whether there were good reasons for her faith—her faith, after all, was what had made her so depressed—but whether there were even good reasons to go on living.

"I just don't trust God anymore," she told me.

"Why not?" I asked.

"Why should I?" she replied.

"Well, look at all He's done for you in Christ. Look at the promises in His Word. He's never lied to you, has He?"

"How should I know?"

"What do you mean?" I asked.

"How do I know He hasn't been lying all along, just playing some great, cosmic joke on all of us, setting everything up so that it *looks* like the gospel's true, but in reality it isn't?"

"Where in the world did you get that idea?"

"Nothing about God convinces me otherwise."

"What do you mean?"

"Suppose He's kept His promises so far," she said. "That doesn't mean He's going to keep doing it. You can't limit God. He's free. And if He's free, then He could turn His back on all His promises anytime. He might have done it already, and we just don't know it. In fact, He might never have meant any of His promises in the first place."

"But in Malachi 3:6 God said, 'I, the LORD, do not change.' God doesn't change, Judy."

"Sure, so long as He doesn't change His mind. But what then?"

"Judy, where in the world did you get these ideas?" I asked. I was bewildered. I'd counseled people with all kinds of doubts about Christ and the gospel, yet I'd never run into someone who professed to be a Christian yet could say things like this.

Judy went on to tell me she hadn't believed this way when she'd begun her Christian walk but had been taught this during several years of training in the youth mission organization with which she'd served in Switzerland. As we talked, she mentioned several other beliefs she'd picked up there that were inconsistent with biblical Christianity—although she had been taught they weren't.

"Judy, you must be misunderstanding something. No Christian mission organization would teach those things," I said. "Do you have any written materials you can bring in here so we can go over them together? Maybe I can help you understand them."

She said she did, and she promised to bring them. A few days later she returned, materials in hand. What began as a counseling appointment with a confused, depressed Christian became years of study, correspondence, and publishing on a controversial movement and set of doctrines that strike at the heart of Christianity.

Greg's Story

It never failed. Every time Greg came over, we wound up talking till one or two o'clock in the morning. No matter what else you might say about Greg—ill informed about theology, sometimes arrogant and rude, rough on biblical exegesis and hermeneutics—you couldn't deny that he was tenacious. He knew what he believed, and he was determined to defend it. This night in 1980 was no different.

As so often, he was angry.

"If what you're saying is true," he nearly shouted at me, "then God is nothing but a tyrant. How could He judge us for sin if we're not even *able* to obey the whole law?"

"Greg, listen," I said. "The Bible says God made mankind good originally but gave him the ability to choose between obedience and disobedience. Adam chose disobedience, and as the whole human race was in him at the time, his choice was our choice. Not only that, his choice corrupted human nature, so that everything Adam became afterward was passed down to every human being since then—except Jesus, whose virgin birth shielded him from the inheritance of sin. Sin now is part of our corrupted nature. It isn't just individual choices we make; it's part of who and what we are. Our individual sins are mere expressions of sin in our hearts. That's why we can't reform ourselves and become acceptable to God."

"Then you're telling me God condemns us for something we're not responsible for? That's blasphemous! I'll never believe that! If we aren't free, then we aren't accountable for our sins, and you're telling me we aren't free. Adam's sin set the course of history off so that everyone is born into a world with sin and temptation, and that makes it easy for people to choose sin, but it doesn't make it necessary. Each of us is responsible for his own sin, not for someone else's."

"So you're saying that we're condemned solely for our own individual sins, not at all for Adam's sin?"

"Right. God couldn't condemn us for someone else's sin."

"And Adam's sin didn't make us sinners but only made it easier for us to choose to sin?"

"Exactly. We wouldn't be responsible if we were bound to sin." Greg figured maybe at last he was making some headway.

"So from birth on, at every moment of our lives, each of us has the inherent ability to choose to obey rather than to disobey God, and there's nothing inevitable about our ever sinning the first time or ever again?"

"Right."

"But Greg, look at what the Bible says. We're not talking here about disagreements among various branches of Christianity. We're talking about something on which Christianity has been unanimous through the centuries. Roman Catholic, Eastern Orthodox, Protestant. Lutheran, Calvinist, Arminian, Wesleyan. They've all said the same thing. And they've said it because—"

"Don't try to impress me with big names," Greg interrupted. "I don't care who they are—Augustine, Luther, Calvin, Wesley—those guys were all mindless idiots if they taught what you're saying."

Greg's arrogance disturbed me again. How could anyone completely ignore nearly two thousand years of church history, filled with creeds and councils and learned treatises on theology by people whose knowledge of the Scriptures dwarfed his and mine put together? But he'd been told by teachers he respected that these men had ignored the plain message of Scripture. And besides, that wasn't the point of the argument. There'd be time later, I hoped, to help him appreciate the importance of church history's contribution to our understanding of the Bible. Right now the important thing was to focus on what the Bible itself said.

"If you'd ever bother to read some of what those 'mindless idiots' wrote, you might think otherwise, Greg. But I didn't bring them up to prove my point, just to keep us both aware how important this issue is. If you're right, Christianity through the ages has been wrong. But they believed what they believed with good reason: it's what the Bible clearly says. Look here again, at Romans 5: '. . . by the transgression of the one the many died. . . . the judgment arose from one transgression resulting in condemnation. . . . by the transgression of the one, death reigned through the one. . . . through one transgression there resulted condemnation to all men. . . .' And look at this one, Greg. Here's the clincher: '. . . *through one man's disobedience the many were made sinners.*' They were *made sinners*, Greg. They sinned because they were sinners; they weren't sinners because they sinned."

"But it can't mean that. That would mean we're not responsible for our sin. You can only be condemned for sin that you freely choose."

"That's not what the Bible says, Greg. And it's a question of whether you believe the Bible or not."

"But it just doesn't make sense."

"Okay, Greg. Which are you going to follow as the supreme teaching authority? Your measly little mind, or the minds of your teachers, or the Bible?"

"The Bible, but—"

"Then look at what the Bible *says*, Greg! '. . . through one man's disobedience the many were *made* sinners'!"

For the first time in hours Greg was silent. I let him sit and think a while, and then I returned to a subject we'd discussed before. Perhaps now, I thought, he'll finally see the connection.

"Greg, listen. You're upset because you think this means you're unfairly condemned for someone else's sin. Never mind for now that your own sin has been quite adequate for your eternal condemnation anyway. The Bible says your very nature was corrupted by Adam's choice, so that you were spiritually dead, enslaved to sin from the moment of your conception. Your own sins were the mere working out in specific circumstances of the very root of your being, and that root in itself was 'dead in trespasses and sins,' 'a child of disobedience,' 'by nature a child of wrath,' just as I showed you in Ephesians 2 two hours ago.

"Now, you may find that hard to swallow, Greg. But it's what the Bible says, and besides, if you don't swallow that, then if you're consistent you'll never swallow what the Bible says about salvation."

"What do you mean?" he asked.

"It's in the same passage in Romans 5," I said, "woven all through what Paul says about sin. But it's especially clear right here, in verse 19: 'For as through the one man's disobedience the many were made sinners, even so through the obedience of the One the many will be made righteous.' You can't reject your inheritance, as a human being, of sin and condemnation from Adam without rejecting your inheritance, as a believer, of righteousness from Christ, Greg."

"But we've argued that point before, Cal. You know I don't believe that."

"Precisely. You've told me, just as you've been taught, that we're kidding ourselves if we think God credits Christ's righteousness to us and therefore sees in us not our sin but His righteousness when He looks at us."

"Exactly."

"What I'm showing you here is that the Bible says the opposite."

"It does not!"

"It does too! And the two hang together."

"You're crazy!"

"Just as all who are in Adam—which includes every human being born naturally—were made sinners and so condemned to death, so all who are in Christ—which includes every believer—were made righteous and so justified to life. That's why Paul says in Romans 3 that there is a 'righteousness of God' that comes to us 'through faith in Jesus Christ for all who believe.' Our righteousness in God's sight can't be our own, Greg. All our righteousnesses are like filthy rags in God's sight. We were made sinners by Adam's sinfulness passed on to us in our corrupted human nature; that's the bad news. The good news is that we are made righteous in God's sight by Christ's righteousness passed on to us in a renewed human nature."

The argument continued for two more hours. Greg wasn't giving in. But something was happening. Something that had been happening since the first of our meetings. He was seeing that the ideas he'd been told were idiotic and without scriptural basis weren't. And this night, he finally took up my challenge to borrow Charles Hodge's *Commentary on Romans* and read it for himself.

"If he's as stupid as you've been told, Greg, you have nothing to worry about. You'll see right through his arguments. If not—well, you'll have to decide what to think."[1]

Ideas Have Consequences

What ties these two incidents, separated by four years and dealing with different doctrinal problems, together? How were this depressed young woman and this fervent young man linked?

Both had been trained in the same youth missionary or-

---

[1] "Judy" is a fictitious name, and some details of her story here are contrived, but she represents a real person who came to me at CRI with the very problems described here. Greg is Greg Robertson, whose testimony may be read in Alan W. Gomes's *Lead Us Not Into Deception: A Biblical Examination of Moral Government Theology*, 3d ed. (La Mirada, CA: published by the author, 1986). The precise wording of the conversation here is contrived, but Greg could testify today that this is substantially how our conversations went.

ganization; both consequently were adherents of the same doctrinal system, whose effects on them psychologically were different but whose underlying elements were consistent. Not officially embraced by any large denomination or parachurch organization, the system has made serious inroads into at least one well-known parachurch organization and has spawned a ministry and publication dedicated to its promotion and defense.[2] The system of doctrine is paradoxically old and new. Its elements are old;[3] how they are tied together into a complete structure is new.

The system's major proponents have dubbed it Moral Government Theology. But today's Moral Government Theology is a far cry from what went by that name two centuries ago, when people as diverse as Jonathan Edwards (a firm Calvinist) and John Wesley (a firm Arminian) both used it to refer to God's government of moral agents through His moral law as contrasted with His government of the physical creation through physical law. Some proponents of contemporary Moral Government Theology claim that it is simply a version of Wesleyan Arminianism. Hence, they reason, opposition to it merely divides the Body of Christ over nonessential doctrines and is therefore unhealthy and unscriptural.

Not so. Moral Government Theology is neither Armin-

---

[2] Dedicated to its defense is Evangelistic Education Ministries, Rockford, Illinois, publishers of *Notes & Quotes*, a newsletter "Proclaiming the Moral Government of God," edited by Dean Harvey. Several other ministries that promote Moral Government Theology are Campus Ministry U.S.A., Newark, Ohio; Destiny Ministries, Frankfurt, Kentucky; Faith Tech Ministries & International Bible Schools, Lansing, Michigan; Revival Theology Promotion, North St. Paul, Minnesota; and Trumpet of Zion Ministries, Lovejoy, Georgia. I am grateful to Bryan R. Cross for informing me about some of these organizations.

[3] It combines some of the teachings of the fifth-century monk Pelagius, who was opposed principally by Augustine and condemned by the ecumenical councils of Carthage (A.D. 418) and Ephesus (A.D. 431), the sixteenth-century philosopher Faustus Socinus, the nineteenth-century revivalist Charles G. Finney, and various others.

ian nor Wesleyan but is outside the range of biblical Christianity. The controversy is not between two brands of Christianity but between Christianity and non-Christianity.

The Rise of Moral Government Theology

Contemporary Moral Government Theology is principally the brainchild of the late Gordon C. Olson, an engineer and informal Bible teacher long associated with Men for Missions. During the 1930s and 1940s, Olson conducted studies that led him to believe God's foreknowledge was necessarily limited by human free will. Those studies, in turn, led to others that persuaded him that the classical doctrines of original sin, human depravity and moral inability, the atonement, and justification were as wrong as the classical doctrine of foreknowledge.

Olson read heavily in the writings of some late nineteenth-century theologians, like Charles McCabe, who had taken the ideas of James Arminius and John Wesley about human freedom farther than their famous forebears ever had. More important, he was impressed by the theological writings of the famous nineteenth-century revivalist Charles G. Finney—whose theology, whatever might be said for his revival tactics, drew stern and powerful criticism for its exaltation of philosophy over Scripture.[4] Olson wove together those ideas

[4] Finney's *Lectures on Theology* suffered a devastating critique in Charles Hodge's review in *Biblical Repository and Princeton Review* 19 (April 1847), reprinted in Hodge's *Selections of Essays and Reviews from the Princeton Review* (1857). The first of the two-part review is reprinted in *The Princeton Theology 1812-1921: Scripture, Science, and Theological Method from Archibald Alexander to Benjamin Breckinridge Warfield*, ed. Mark A. Noll (Grand Rapids: Baker, 1983), 166-75. As Noll points out in introducing Hodge's review, "Hodge contended that Finney's theology was really an exercise in specious deductive reasoning. He began with erroneous assumptions and spun these out with blatant disregard for Scripture and Christian experience. . . . Finney in fact reasons precisely this way." Noll adds in a foot-

with some of his own, and the eventual result was what he began to call Moral Government Theology.

During the 1960s and 1970s, Olson and an associate, Harry Conn, another engineer, began to teach Moral Government Theology for various mission organizations, often in recruiting, motivating, or training young people. Moral Government Theology (MGT) first began to spread rapidly when Olson and Conn became regular speakers for Youth With a Mission (YWAM), which has since become one of the larger youth missionary organizations in the world. Contrary to YWAM's repeated denials that MGT was an important part of its teaching, it was in YWAM training that Judy and Greg—like thousands of others from the late 1970s through the 1980s, and some even into the 1990s—learned MGT.[5]

---

note, "For example, early in the *Lectures* Finney argued extensively that moral obligations pertain, in a strict sense, only to intentions. At the end of his reasoning he added, 'The Bible everywhere either expressly or implicitly recognizes this truth.'" We shall see that the prime theorizer of contemporary Moral Government Theology, Gordon Olson, does the same. Asahel Nettleton, another preacher of Finney's day whom God used greatly in sending revival, conducted a running battle with Finney in oral and written debates, described well in John Thornbury's "Asahel Nettleton's Conflict with Finneyism," *Baptist Reformation Review*, Summer 1977 (reprint: P.O. Box 40161, Nashville: Baptist Reformation Review, n.d.). See also Benjamin Breckinridge Warfield, "The Theology of Charles G. Finney," in his *Perfectionism*, ed. Samuel G. Craig (Philadelphia: Presbyterian and Reformed, 1974), pp. 166-215. For a thorough contrast between Finney's ideas of revival as generated by man's design and the classical idea of revival as sent by God as an outpouring of His Spirit—a view that dominated the Reformation and was shared by the great seventeenth-century leaders in Revival of every theological persuasion, including the Arminian Methodist John Wesley, the Calvinist Methodist George Whitefield, the Calvinist Congregationalist Jonathan Edwards, and the Calvinist Presbyterian Samuel Davies—see Iain H. Murray, *Revival & Revivalism: The Making and Marring of American Evangelicalism 1750-1858* (Edinburgh, Scotland, and Carlisle, PA: Banner of Truth Trust, 1994).

[5] YWAM's only official, public response to criticisms about its allowing MGT to be taught under its auspices has been "A Statement About Moral Government by Youth With a Mission," signed by YWAM President and Founder Loren Cunningham and Executive Director Floyd

While MGT writers have published principally through small publishers outside the mainstream of evangelicalism, similar views, especially regarding God's omniscience, have begun to be promoted in books published by mainstream evangelical publishing houses. The publication of a largely philosophical assault on God's absolute foreknowledge that owes much to Process Theology, Richard Rice's *God's Foreknowledge and Man's Free Will*, by Bethany Fellowship (1980, 1985) was alarming. More recently, Bethany continued in the same vein by publishing Winkie Pratney's *The Nature and Character of God* (1988). Most alarming has been the publication of *The Grace of God, The Will of Man: A Case for Arminianism*, edited by Clark Pinnock, by Zondervan/ Academie Books (1989)—a book that goes well beyond the agenda suggested by its subtitle. All of these books challenge not Calvinism merely but the orthodox doctrine of God's omniscience shared equally by Eastern Orthodoxy, Roman Catholicism (Augustinian, Scholastic, Tridentine, and modern), Lutheranism, Calvinism, Arminianism, and Wesleyanism.

McClung Jr. (December 7, 1988), in which the authors admit to YWAM's having fallen "into a spirit of theological argumentativeness" over MGT but never come to grips with the substantive doctrinal issues, insisting instead that to whatever extent MGT was taught in YWAM it was simply a Wesleyan view and that only narrow-minded Calvinists who refused to recognize the orthodoxy of anything but Calvinism were critical of it. Unofficially, in a variety of ways, YWAM has denied that MGT ever was taught prevalently in the organization. But for thorough documentation that MGT has been a widespread and often central element of YWAM training, see Gomes, *Lead Us Not Into Deception*, Appendices A and B. Because the purpose of this book is not to evaluate YWAM itself but to assess MGT, we will not do the former here. Suffice it to say that at least during the 1970s and the early 1980s, MGT was the dominant theological perspective at every YWAM training base around the world that Gomes and I, with the help of many contacts both inside and outside YWAM, were able to check, and that many of YWAM's most respected and powerful teachers, both on and off staff, taught it, according to first-hand testimony by YWAM students.

Although Conn and others have published on MGT,[6] Olson's writings and taped lectures have been definitive of the system and most important in the movement.[7] For that reason, most of this analysis will focus on Olson's writings.[8]

Because each of the three following chapters was written originally to stand alone in a different context, there is significant overlap among them. However, each approaches MGT from a different perspective and with a different focus, and it is hoped that their doing so will lend greater clarity to the debate and strength to the orthodox arguments.

---

[6] *E.g.*, Harry Conn, *Four Trojan Horses* (Nyack, NY: Parson Publishing, 1978), especially chapter 3 and appendices 1-2; Harry Conn, ed., *Finney's Systematic Theology* (Minneapolis: Bethany Fellowship, 1976); Howard Roy Elseth, *Did God Know?* (St. Paul: Calvary United Church, 1977); Winkie Pratney, *Youth Aflame*, (place and publisher unlisted, 1970; rev. ed., Minneapolis: Bethany Fellowship, 1983); Winkie Pratney, *The Nature and Character of God: The Magnificent Doctrine of God in Understandable Language* (Minneapolis: Bethany Fellowship, 1988); George Otis Jr., *The God They Never Knew* (Van Nuys, CA: Bible Voice Publishers, 1978). Also important is a tape series, "The Moral Government of God," by Harry Conn, produced for some time by YWAM.

[7] Most important among Olson's writings has been his evangelism training manual, *Sharing Your Faith: The 3 M's of Witnessing—The Messenger, The Message, The Method*, 4th rev. ed. (Chicago: Bible Research Fellowship, 1976), republished with very little alteration as *The Truth Shall Make You Free* (Franklin Park, IL: Bible Research Fellowship, 1980; also once copyrighted and printed by Truth Press International, a YWAM agency in Hurlach, West Germany). This manual, under both titles, was heavily used in YWAM's Discipleship Training Schools and Schools of Evangelism at YWAM bases around the world. Also very important was a forty-tape lecture series on Moral Government by Olson, produced and distributed by YWAM under the title "The Messenger, the Message and Method of Sharing Your Faith." Other important publications by Olson include *The Entrance of Sin Into the World* (Minneapolis: Men for Missions, 1973), *Holiness and Sin* (Minneapolis: Men for Missions, 1971), and *The Moral Government of God*, 3d rev. ed. (1966; Minneapolis: Men for Missions, 1974).

[8] For extensive citations from the writings of other MGT proponents, see chapters 2 and 3.

Chapter One

Root and Branches: The Main Ideas of Moral Government Theology

At the root of MGT lies a philosophical assumption about freedom. According to Gordon Olson, "The power to the contrary is essential to free agency—A free moral agent may always act contrary to any influence, not destructive to his freedom, that may be brought to bear upon him."[1] "Voluntary responsible action involves the possibility of non-compliance or of contrary choice—the freedom of uncertainty. Virtuous action must be voluntary action. If no contrary choice, then no virtuous choice. . . ."[2] No choice may be called virtuous, then, unless the one who made it might just as well have chosen the opposite. Add to this philosophical definition of freedom the assertion that God and man are inherently free, and important doctrines necessarily follow.

First, man is born morally neutral and is always capable of choosing whether to sin. Olson insists that man has "ability of intellect," "ability of emotion," and "ability of free will or self-determination"; that "Holiness and sin are free volun-

[1] Gordon C. Olson, *Sharing Your Faith: The 3 M's of Witnessing—The Messenger, the Message, the Method*, 4th rev. ed., p. W-Me-IV-7. (Olson uses this page numbering system in both *Sharing* and *The Truth Shall Make You Free.*)

[2] Olson, *The Truth Shall Make You Free*, p. T-V-1. (*The Truth Shall Make You Free* is largely a rewrite of *Sharing Your Faith.*)

tary acts of will or states of mind, and, although strongly influenced, are not caused by any internal force of nature, tendency, or instinct"; that "Sin is not . . . an abstract thing which invades and lodges somewhere in our personalities, but is rather an orderly sequence of wrong choices and conduct"; that "Depravity strongly influences, but does not compel, toward wrong action. We choose to follow our inclinations when we sin"; that "Moral depravity . . . is always a voluntary development which results from the wrong choices of our wills"; that "The universality of sin in the world is not to be accounted for, therefore, by some fixed causation in our personality inherited by birth"; that "So-called inability is a question of 'will not' rather than 'cannot' obey God's reasonable requirements."[3]

Hence, each person is condemned only for his own sin. For Olson, ". . . a contradiction would exist in the Bible if any statement could be found declaring our guilt for Adam's sin."[4] "If the Bible affirmed that we are held accountable for other's (*sic*) sins, and particularly for Adam's sin, this would become such a gross injustice in the economy of God as to erect a barrier to intelligent thought and the meaning of guilt."[5] Why? Because "All sin consists in sinning–there can be no moral character but in moral acts."[6]

Second, man's future free choices cannot be foreknown by God; for them to be so would be for them not to be free. The "future choices of moral beings," Olson writes, "when acting freely in their moral agency, have not been brought into existence as yet and thus are not fixities or objects of possible knowledge."[7] Thus, "Many Bible passages, when taken in their natural meaning, appear to indicate that God

---

[3] Olson, *Truth*, pp. T-IV-2; T-V-1; T-V-3; T-VI-5-6; *Sharing*, pp. W-Me-IV-4-5; W-Me-VIII-6.

[4] Olson, *Sharing*, p. W-Me-IV-5.

[5] *Ibid.*, p. W-Me-VII-3.

[6] *Ibid.*, unnumbered page opposite W-Me-IV-6.

[7] Olson, *Truth*, p. T-III-13.

does not have absolute foreknowledge over all his own future actions, nor over all those of His moral creatures."[8] Therefore God's foreknowledge is limited, and He learns new things as people make choices.

Third, the principle of contrary choice "applies to actions of the Godhead as well as to the self-caused actions of men."[9] Therefore: (1) God cannot foreknow His own future choices, for if He did then He would not make those choices freely, and He would cease to be a moral agent. (2) God's moral character, like man's, depends constantly on His choices.

> Moral attributes involve the element of choice, or have a voluntary causation to them. They are not natural attributes in that they are not endowments of God's existence, but are moral in the sense that they are the result of a disposition of will. They exist *because each Member of the Godhead perpetually chooses that they should be so*. Moral character must be an active something. It cannot be a static fixity of some sort back of the will, causing its actions.[10]

Hence the absolutely unfettered will, not the moral nature, lies at the root of God's (or any moral agent's) choices and character. This follows necessarily from Olson's first principle, already cited: "Voluntary responsible action involves the possibility of non-compliance or of contrary choice—the freedom of uncertainty. . . . If no contrary choice, then no virtuous choice. . . ."[11]

The shocking implication of this last idea—that God is morally changeable—might appear to contradict another of Olson's statements: "God's nature and moral character imposes limitations. God is able to do whatever He wills (except with moral beings), but His will is limited to doing those things which are in harmony with His wise and holy

[8] *Ibid.*, p. T-III-18.
[9] *Ibid.*, p. T-III-13.
[10] *Ibid.*, p. T-III-23, emphasis added.
[11] *Ibid.*, p. T-V-1.

and perfect character. God cannot do things contrary to Himself. This is not a defect in Divine omnipotence but a perfection of the Divine Being."[12] But Olson chooses his terms carefully. God's *character*, he says, like all moral character, "must be an active something. It cannot be a static fixity of some sort back of the will, causing its actions. Moral character is dynamic; it is the whole personality in action; it is what we are doing with our endowments or abilities of personality and the moral understanding which we possess."[13] If it is true that Olson believes that God's "*will* is limited to doing those things which are in harmony with His wise and holy and perfect *character*,"[14] it is also true that Olson believes that God's *character* "cannot be a static fixity of some sort back of the will, causing its actions" but "is the whole personality in action; it is what [God is] doing with [His] endowments or abilities of personality and the moral understanding which [He] possess[es]."[15] "*Moral attributes*," Olson insists, "involve the element of choice, or have a voluntary causation to them. They are not natural attributes in that they are not endowments of God's existence, but are moral in the sense that they *are the result of a disposition of will*. They exist because each Member of the Godhead perpetually chooses that they should be so."[16]

So while God's "will is limited to doing those things which are in harmony with His wise and holy and perfect character," this can only be so as long as His character remains wise and holy and perfect, and nothing can guarantee that it will do so forever, for character by definition "cannot be a static fixity," and must "involve the element of choice, or have a voluntary causation" to it, must—in short—be "the result of a disposition of will." As Olson puts it, "*The will determines the*

[12] *Ibid.*, p. T-III-22.
[13] *Ibid.*, p. T-III-23.
[14] *Ibid.*, p. T-III-22, emphases added.
[15] *Ibid.*, p. T-III-23.
[16] *Ibid.*, emphases added.

nature or character, rather than the nature the will."[17] Should God ever choose to make His character other than wise and holy and perfect—and no "internal force of nature" can prevent His doing so—why, then of course that wise and holy and perfect character will no longer limit what He wills; a different sort of character will do so.[18] To put it simply, we have no assurance that God will not decide tomorrow to become the devil.

Not only God's knowledge and moral character but even His power collapses before the inexorable implications of human autonomy in MGT. Olson hints at this in a parenthetical phrase in his statement of the limits on God's will, cited above: "God is able to do whatever He wills *(except with moral beings)*, but His will is limited to doing those things which are in harmony with His wise and holy and perfect character."[19] He makes it explicit when he writes, "Man as an endowed moral being has been given the ability to *limit the omnipotence of God* in his sphere of life. Mankind by their rebellion against God and their obstinacy in refusing the mercy and forgiveness through the atoning death of Christ have imposed very great limitations upon God's will and happiness. . . . God in creating moral creatures with *the power of contrary choice* made this a possibility."[20]

Ideas have consequences. The true stories that introduced this book flowed inexorably from Olson's ideas about freedom and their implications for man and God. Judy stopped trusting a God whose moral character she could no longer depend on; Greg proudly insisted on making the human will autonomous—even at the expense of losing the wonderful

---

[17] Olson, *Holiness and Sin*, p. 24, emphasis added.

[18] The inherent inconsistency in Olson's system is evident here. On one page he makes the will dependent on the character; on the next page he makes the character dependent on the will. Such elementary deficiencies in logic and analysis are abundant in Olson's writings.

[19] Olson, *Truth*, p. T-III-22, emphasis added.

[20] *Ibid.*, emphases added.

biblical promise of gracious justification by the crediting of Christ's righteousness to believing sinners.

For the implications build. If—since the power of contrary choice is essential to free agency—"Holiness and sin are free voluntary acts of will or states of mind, and, although strongly influenced, are not caused by any internal force of nature, tendency, or instinct," and "Sin is not . . . an abstract thing which invades and lodges somewhere in our personalities, but is rather an orderly sequence of wrong choices and conduct," then it follows that our being righteous in God's sight cannot be a matter of Christ's righteousness being credited to our account instead of our sin.

Since Olson explicitly denies that man inherits sin or guilt from Adam (*i.e.*, he denies the doctrine of original sin—the imputation of Adam's sin and guilt to his posterity), it should come as no surprise that he also denies the imputation of Christ's righteousness to believers, finding the cause of salvation not in Christ's atoning death but in the believer's self-reformation: "Romans 5:12-19 does not establish the dogma of the literal imputation of Adam's sin to all his posterity, but merely affirms in a parallelism that just as Adam's sin was the *occasion, not cause*, of the voluntary disobedience of all men, so Christ is the *occasion, not cause*, of the salvation offered to all men."[21] "The active obedience or holiness of Christ . . . is not legally imputed to the believer."[22] And if Christ's righteousness is not credited to the believer, neither is the believer's sin credited to Christ on the cross. For sin is not a principle; sins are isolated, individual acts only.

But if our sins are not borne by Christ on the cross, how are we to be freed from the penalty due them? Ah, the question assumes that a penalty is due, but none is!

> A voluntary disposition of mercy and forgiveness prevails equally among all the Members of the Godhead. The

[21] *Ibid.*, p. T-VI-8, emphasis added.

[22] Olson, *Sharing*, "Historical Opinions," p. 2.

> Godhead are without personal vindictiveness. The problems of forgiveness are not personal but governmental. God does not require an exact payment for sin to satisfy retributive justice, but only requires that an atonement shall satisfy public justice and all the problems of a full and free reconciliation in His government of moral beings.[23]

This denial of any demand for the satisfaction of retributive (or vindictive) justice in God leads Olson to deny that Christ's atoning death was the true payment of a penalty to satisfy the justice of God:

> The sacrifice of Christ is not the payment of a debt, nor is it a complete satisfaction of justice for sin. It is a Divinely-appointed condition which precedes the forgiveness of sin, just as the death of a lamb or a goat in the Mosaic economy. Christ's sufferings *took the place of a penalty*, so that His sufferings have the same effect in reconciling God to man, and procuring the forgiveness of sin, that the sinner's endurance of the punishment due to his sins would have had. The sufferings of Christ were *not a substituted penalty, but a substitute for a penalty*.[24]

The atonement of Christ "[r]endered satisfaction to public justice (a demonstration before all that rebellion against authority will be punished), as distinguished from retributive or vindictive justice."[25]

Here is MGT in a nutshell:

• Freedom entails the power of contrary choice, and God and man are both free.

• God is finite, imperfect, and changeable in his knowledge, character, and power, and He does not require vengeance for sin.

---

[23] Olson, *Truth*, p. T-VII-4.

[24] Olson, "Historical Opinions as to the Nature of Christ's Atoning Death," 3, in *Truth*, page following T-VII-10, emphases added.

[25] Olson, *Truth*, p. T-VIII-4.

• Man is perfectly free—his freedom implies that he cannot have inherited either sin or a morally corrupt nature from Adam, and it necessarily limits God's knowledge, will, and power.

• The gospel is that "the atoning death of Christ," as Olson deigns to call it—nay, even Christ Himself—"is the occasion, not cause, of the salvation offered to all men."[26] The "consequences of right and wrong moral action" in MGT ". . . are based *solely upon personal merit or demerit* as known only to God" and "are and will be in exact accord or in proportion to merit and demerit."[27]

By starting with the definition of freedom as the "power of contrary choice" Olson is forced ultimately to deny nearly the whole defining body of Christian faith: original sin, unregenerate man's moral inability, the imputation of Christ's righteousness in justification (parallel to the imputation of Adam's sin in condemnation), the substitutionary and satisfactory atonement for sin in Christ's death, and the moral and intellectual infinity, perfection, and immutability of God. And just like Finney before him—only going to greater extremes—Olson reaches his conclusions not on the basis of Scripture but by inferences from philosophical assumptions. What might Olson have found had he subjected his first principle and his inferences to the light of Scripture?

Human Freedom and Sin in Scripture

Scripture knows nothing of freedom as the "power of contrary choice." Such a view is rooted in an autonomous notion of man. Rather, Scripture contrasts freedom with bondage to sin. Real freedom is not autonomy but deliverance *from* the slavery to sin in which all men are born, *into* the

[26] *Ibid.*, p. T-VI-8.
[27] *Ibid.*, pp. T-IV-10-11.

glorious freedom of the children of God: "But thanks be to God that though you *were* slaves of sin, you became obedient from the heart to that form of teaching to which you were committed, and having been freed from sin, you became slaves of righteousness" (Rom. 6:17-18, emphasis added). God did not make man to be his own lord—to be autonomous. Try as he might, man never can escape being Number Two; he must always be someone's slave. The serpent's trickery was to make Adam and Eve think that by disobeying God they could begin to rule their own lives—they could be Number One; instead, rejecting God's rule only meant embracing Satan's (Eph. 2:2). "But now having been freed from sin and enslaved to God, you derive your benefit, resulting in sanctification, and the outcome, eternal life. For the wages of sin is death, but the free gift of God is eternal life in Christ Jesus our Lord" (Rom. 6:22-23).

Far from human freedom's being the "power of contrary choice," the very exercise of that power robbed human beings of the only freedom for which we were made: the freedom of obedience to our rightful Sovereign. And no "power of contrary choice" in us will ever free us from sin's tyranny, for we are "dead in trespasses and sins" and "by nature children of wrath" (Eph. 2:1, 3). We suffer, as Luther put it in the title of one of his most famous books, from *The Bondage of the Will*; our wills are bound to our corrupt, rebellious, sinful nature inherited from Adam.[28]

---

[28] Martin Luther, *The Bondage of the Will*, trans. Henry Cole (Grand Rapids, MI: Baker, 1976), also in *Luther and Erasmus: Free Will and Salvation*, ed. E. Gordon Rupp and Philip S. Watson (Library of Christian Classics: Ichthus Edition; Philadelphia, PA: Westminster, 1969). An important distinction is to be made between *free will* and *free agency*. No *will* is free, for every will is bound by the nature of the person to whom it belongs. But *agents* (or selves) are free who choose their own acts rather than being forced to do them by someone or something outside themselves. Space does not permit more thorough discussion of this point here. Interested readers should see Charles Hodge, *Systematic Theology*, 3 volumes (Grand Rapids, MI: Eerdmans, 1973 reprint), 2:290-299 and chapter 2 of this work.

What we need is not a free will but a new, holy, obedient, righteous nature (2 Cor. 5:17) to which our will is bound. And we cannot produce that new nature for ourselves—least of all by an act of our own will, which is bound by the contrary nature. Dead, rebellious men do not—cannot—repent, believe, and reform their lives. "But God, being rich in mercy, because of His great love with which He loved us, *even when we were dead in our transgressions*, made us alive together with Christ (by grace you have been saved), and raised us up with Him, and seated us with Him in the heavenly places, in Christ Jesus, in order that in the ages to come He might show the surpassing riches of His grace in kindness toward us in Christ Jesus. For by grace you have been saved through faith; and that not of yourselves, it is the gift of God; not as a result of works, that no one should boast. For we are His workmanship, created in Christ Jesus for good works, which God prepared beforehand, that we should walk in them" (Eph. 2:4-10, emphasis added).

Divine Knowledge, Holiness, and Justice in Scripture

And far from divine freedom's being the "power of contrary choice," God's freedom is precisely that He never will or even can do anything contrary to His holy and good nature. "Thou *art good* and *doest good*" (Ps. 119:68).[29] That is why God "cannot lie" (Tit. 1:2); why we know that His promise and His purpose are "unchangeable" and therefore that "it is *impossible* for God to lie" (Heb. 6:17-18, emphasis added); why God could rest His assurance to Israel on His own immutability when He said, "For I, the LORD, do not change; therefore you, O sons of Jacob, are not consumed" (Mal. 3:6); why we

[29] Scripture distinguishes *being* good from *doing* good (just as it distinguishes *being* sinful from *doing* sin). God's goodness is inherent to His nature, and His good actions flow from it (just as man's sinfulness is inherent to his fallen nature, and His sinful actions flow from it).

can be comforted to know that "If we are faithless, He remains faithful; for He cannot deny Himself" (2 Tim. 2:13). After all, "God is not a man, that He should lie, nor a son of man, that He should repent; has He said, and will He not do it? Or has He spoken, and will He not make it good?" (Num. 23:19).

Like His nature, so also God's knowledge is perfect, admitting no improvement. "God . . . knows all things" (1 John 3:20). Not just some things; not all things *except* those that "have not been brought into existence as yet and thus are not fixities or objects of possible knowledge"—Olson's description of the future choices of free moral agents acting in their moral agency.[30] The God who "calls those things which do not exist as though they did" (Rom. 4:17) "knows *all* things." Nothing can be hid from God (Ps. 139:11-12; Heb. 4:13). "His understanding is infinite" (Ps. 147:5), and what is infinite cannot grow, for if it did, it would be greater after its growth than before, which would prove that it was not infinite before. Hence God's knowledge can never increase (Isa. 40:13-14), for it is already all-comprehensive. God's knowledge is absolutely comprehensive (1) in space (2 Chron. 16:9; Ps. 139:1-2, 6-10); (2) in time (Ps. 139:15-16; Is. 41:21-26; John 13:19); (3) in scope, including all things from the greatest to the least (Ps. 147:4; Job 31:4; Ps. 139:2-4; Matt. 10:30); and (4) not only in things actual (what is or will be) but also in things contingent (what could be, on any supposition, whether actual or not) (1 Sam. 23:10-13; Ps. 81:13-16; Jer. 38:17-18; *cf.* 19-23; Matt. 11:20-24).

And this God of infinite and unchangeable knowledge and holiness is also a God of perfect justice who—contrary to Olson—*does* demand vengeance on sin. "I, the LORD your God, am a jealous God, visiting the iniquity of the fathers on the children, on the third and the fourth generations of those who hate Me . . ." (Ex. 20:5; *cf.* Ex. 20:7; Deut. 29:19-20; 32:35; Josh. 24:19-20; Nah. 1:2-3; Rom. 12:19).

---

[30] Olson, *Truth*, p. T-III-13.

The Gospel of Redemption and Justification

But thank God that although "all have sinned and fall short of the glory of God," we are "justified as a gift by His grace through the redemption which is in Christ Jesus; whom God displayed publicly as a *propitiation*[31] in His blood through faith. This was to demonstrate His righteousness, because in the forbearance of God He passed over the sins previously committed; for the demonstration, I say, of His righteousness at the present time, that He might be just and the justifier of the one who has faith in Jesus" (Rom. 3:23-26).

And this redemption by Christ is truly a *payment* of our penalty for sin, Olson's denials notwithstanding: "[Y]ou were not redeemed[32] with perishable things . . . but with precious[33] blood, as of a lamb unblemished and spotless, the blood of Christ" (1 Pet. 1:18-19). "[T]he Son of Man did not come to be served, but to serve, and to give His life a ransom[34] for many" (Matt. 20:28). "In Him we have redemption[35] through His blood, the forgiveness of our trespasses, according to the riches of His grace" (Eph. 1:7). "[The Holy Spirit] is given as a pledge[36] of our inheritance, with a view to the

---

[31] Greek *hilasterion*, "that which expiates or propitiates," *i.e.*, satisfies the demand for vengeance, "concr. a means of expiation, gift to procure expiation." From *hilasmos*, "expiation, propitiation . . . sin-offering." Walter Bauer, *A Greek-English Lexicon of the New Testament and Other Early Christian Writings*, 2d ed., trans. William F. Arndt and F. Wilbur Gingrich, rev. F. Wilbur Gingrich and Frederick W. Danker (Chicago: University of Chicago Press, 1979), p. 375.

[32] Greek *elutrothete*, from *lutroo*, "to free by paying a ransom, redeem," *Ibid.*, p. 482.

[33] Greek *timio*, "valuable, precious, . . . of great worth or value." From *time*, "set a price on, estimate, value." *Ibid.*, pp. 818, 817.

[34] Greek *lutron*, "price of release, ransom," *Ibid.*, p. 482.

[35] Greek *apolutrosin*, "buying back a slave or captive, making him free by payment of a ransom (*lutron* . . .)," *Ibid.*, p. 96.

[36] Greek *arrabon*, "first instalment, deposit, down payment, pledge, that pays a part of the purchase price in advance, and so secures a legal claim to the article in question," *Ibid.*, p. 109.

redemption[37] of God's own possession" (Eph. 1:14). "[Christ] gave Himself for us, that He might redeem[38] us from every lawless deed" (Titus 2:14). "Worthy art Thou to take the book, and to break its seals; for Thou wast slain, and didst purchase[39] for God with Thy blood men from every tribe and tongue and people and nation" (Rev. 5:9).

In His atoning death, Christ truly substituted Himself for us in bearing the penalty for our sins: "But He was pierced through for our transgressions, He was crushed for our iniquities; the chastening for our well-being fell upon Him, and by His scourging we are healed" (Is. 53:5). He was offered up "to bear the sins of many" (Heb. 9:28), "the just for [that is, "in the stead of, as a substitute for"][40] the unjust" (1 Pet. 3:18), "a ransom[41] for[42] all" who would be saved (1 Tim. 2:6).

Just as surely as He gave Himself to bear our sins, Christ also gives us the gift of His righteousness: "For if by the transgression of the one, death reigned through the one, much more those who receive the abundance of grace and of the gift of righteousness will reign in life through the One, Jesus Christ. So then as through one transgression there resulted condemnation to all men, even so through one act of righ-

---

[37] Greek *apolutrosin*, "buying back a slave or captive, making him free by payment of a ransom," *Ibid.*, p. 96.

[38] Greek *lutrosetai*, from *lutro* , "to free by paying a ransom, redeem," *Ibid.*, p. 482.

[39] Greek *egorasas*, from *agoraz* , "buy, purchase," from *agora*, "market place," *Ibid.*, pp. 12-13.

[40] The Greek word *húper*, here translated *for*, conveys, in contexts like this, the sense of substitution. See A. T. Robertson, *A Grammar of the Greek New Testament in the Light of Historical Research* (Nashville: Broadman Press, 1934), pp. 630-631; A. T. Robertson, *Word Pictures in the New Testament*, 6 vols. (Nashville: Broadman Press, 1933), 6:115-16; R. C. H. Lenski, *The Interpretation of the Epistles of St. Peter, St. John and St. Jude* (Minneapolis: Augsburg, 1966), p. 156; James Hope Moulton and George Milligan, ed., *The Vocabulary of the Greek Testament Illustrated from the Papyri and Other Non-literary Sources* (Grand Rapids: Eerdmans, [1930] 1976), p. 651.

[41] Greek *antílutron*, literally, a substituted payment.

[42] Greek *húper*, in the place of; see the next-to-last note above.

teousness there resulted justification of life to all men. For as through the one man's disobedience the many were made sinners, even so through the obedience of the One the many will be made righteous" (Rom. 5:17-19). By taking our place on the cross, Christ "became to us wisdom from God and righteousness and sanctification, and redemption" (1 Cor. 1:30).

And we obtain this gift of righteousness not by works but solely by faith: ". . . I count all things to be loss in view of the surpassing value of knowing Christ Jesus my Lord, for whom I have suffered the loss of all things, and count them but rubbish in order that I may gain Christ, and may be found in Him, not having a righteousness of my own derived from the Law, but that which is through faith in Christ, the righteousness which comes from God on the basis of faith" (Phil. 3:8-9). "For what does the Scripture say? 'And Abraham believed God, and it was reckoned to him as righteousness.' Now to the one who works, his wage is not reckoned as a favor, but as what is due. But to the one who does not work, but believes in Him who justifies the ungodly, his faith is reckoned as righteousness, just as David also speaks of the blessing upon the man to whom God reckons righteousness apart from works" (Rom. 4:3-6).

Minor Aberration or Departure from the Faith?

Proponents of MGT often depict opposition to it as rooted in "hyper-Calvinism," claiming that their doctrines are nothing but Wesleyan Arminianism, which is recognized in evangelical circles as an orthodox option in theology. Not so.

Neither Wesley nor Arminius would ever have dreamed of denying God's absolute and infinite foreknowledge or His unchangeable goodness. Wesley boldly defended God's foreknowledge in commenting on John 6:64,[43] and both God's

[43] John Wesley, *Explanatory Notes Upon the New Testament*, 15th ed. (New York: Carlton & Porter, n.d.), p. 232.

foreknowledge and His moral immutability in his sermon on "Divine Providence,"[44] and he confidently taught that Christ's "divine righteousness belongs to his divine nature. . . . Now this is his eternal, essential, *immutable*, holiness; his infinite justice, mercy, and truth: in all which, He and the Father are one."[45] And Arminius's words rejecting the notion that God is *freely* good breathe fire:

> . . . [some] brought forward an instance, or example, in which [they alleged that] Necessity and Liberty met together; and that was God, who is both necessarily and freely good. This assertion of theirs displeased me so exceedingly, as to cause me to say, *that it was not far removed from blasphemy*. At this time, I entertain a similar opinion about it; and in a few words I thus prove its *falsity*, *absurdity*, and the *blasphemy* [contained] *in the falsity*. (1.) Its *falsity*. He who by *natural necessity*, and according to his very essence and the whole of his nature, is good, nay, who is Goodness itself, the Supreme Good, the First Good from whom all good proceeds, through whom every good comes, in whom every good exists, and by a participation of whom what things soever have any portion of good in them are good, and more or less good as they are nearer or more remote from it. He is not FREELY good. For it is a contradiction in an adjunct, or an opposition in an apposition. But God is good by natural necessity, according to his entire nature and essence, and is Goodness itself, the supreme and primary Good, from whom, through whom, and in whom is all good, &c. Therefore, **God is not freely good.** (2.) Its *absurdity*. Liberty is an affection of the Divine Will; not of

[44] *By John Wesley: A modern reader's introduction to the man and his message . . .*, ed. T. Otto Nall (New York: Association Press, 1961), pp. 20-21; extract from the sermon "Divine Providence" in *The Works of the Rev. John Wesley*, ed. John Emory (New York and Cincinnati: Methodist Book Concern, 1916; first published in the United States by Emory and Waugh, New York, 1831), 2:99-107.

[45] *By John Wesley*, pp. 62-3; extracted from Wesley's sermon "The Lord of Righteousness," in *Standard Sermons of John Wesley*, ed. E. H. Sugden (London: The Epworth Press, 1921), 2:426-7.

> the Divine Essence, Understanding, or Power; and therefore it is not an affection of the Divine Nature, considered in its totality. It is indeed an effect of the will, according to which it is borne towards an object that is neither primary nor adequate, and that is different from God himself; and this effect of the will, therefore, is posterior in order to that affection of the will according to which God is borne towards a proper, primary and adequate object, which is himself. But Goodness is an affection of the whole of the Divine Nature, Essence, Life, Understanding, Will, Power, &c. Therefore, **God is not freely good;** that is, **he is not good by the mode of liberty, but by that of natural necessity.** . . . (3.) I prove that *blasphemy* is contained in this assertion: because, if God be freely good, (that is, not by nature and natural necessity,) he can be or can be made *not good.* As whatever any one wills freely, he has it in his power *not to will*; and whatever any one does freely, he can refrain from doing. . . . [T]he Christian Fathers justly attached blasphemy to those who said, "the Father begat the Son *willingly*, or by his own will;" because from this it would follow, that the Son had [*principium*] an origin similar to that of the creatures. But with how much greater equity does blasphemy fasten itself upon those who declare, "that God is *freely* good!"[46]

Both Wesley and Arminius clearly affirmed that all men (except Christ) inherit the sin and guilt of Adam and therefore are naturally bound to sin until regenerated by God. "This, therefore, is the first grand distinguishing point between Heathenism and Christianity," wrote Wesley:

> The one acknowledges that many men are infected with many vices, and even born with a proneness to them; but supposes withal, that in some the natural good much over-

[46] Arminius, *Apology Against Thirty-one Defamatory Articles*, Article XXII, in *The Writings of James Arminius*, 3 vols., trans. James Nichols and W. R. Bagnall (Grand Rapids, MI: Baker Book House, 1977), 1:344-6; italicized emphases original, boldfaced emphases added.

> balances the evil: the other declares that all men are "conceived in sin," and "shapen in wickedness"—that hence there is in every man a "carnal mind," which is enmity against God; which is not, cannot be, subject to "his law"; which so infects the whole soul, that "there dwelleth in" him "in his flesh," in his natural state, "no good thing"; but "every imagination of the thoughts of his heart is evil," only evil, and that "continually."
>
> Hence we may learn that all who deny this, call it "original sin," or by any other title, are but Heathens still, in the fundamental point which differences Heathenism from Christianity. They may, indeed, allow, that men have many vices; that some are born with us; and that, consequently, we are not born altogether so wise or so virtuous as we should be; there being few that will roundly affirm, "We are born with as much propensity to good as to evil, and that every man is, by nature as virtuous and wise as Adam was at creation." But here is the shibboleth: Is man by nature filled with all manner of evil? Is he void of all good? Is he wholly fallen? Is his soul totally corrupted? Or, to come back to the text, is "every imagination of the thoughts of his heart only evil continually?"
>
> Allow this, and you are so far a Christian. Deny it, and you are but a Heathen still.[47]

Arminius insisted,

> The proper and immediate effect of [Adam's first] sin was the offending of the Deity. . . . From this violation of his law, God conceives just displeasure, which is the second effect of sin. [Genesis 3:16-19, 23, 24] But to anger succeeds infliction of punishment, which was in this instance twofold. (1.) [*Reatus*] A liability to two deaths. [Genesis 2:17; Romans 6:23] (2.) [*Privatio*] The withdrawing of that primitive righteousness and holiness, which, because they are the effects of the Holy Spirit dwelling in man, ought not

---

[47] *By John Wesley*, pp. 29-30; extracted from Wesley's sermon "Original Sin" in *Standard Sermons of John Wesley*, 2:222-5.

> to have remained in him after he had fallen from the favor of God, and had incurred the Divine displeasure. [Luke 19:26] For this Spirit is a seal of God's favor and good will. [Romans 8:14, 15; 1 Corinthians 2:12] . . . The whole of this sin, however, is not peculiar to our first parents, but is common to the entire race and to all their posterity, who, at the time when this sin was committed, were in their loins, and who have since descended from them by the natural mode of propagation, according to the primitive benediction. For in Adam "all have sinned." [Romans 5:12] Wherefore, whatever punishment was brought down upon our first parents, has likewise pervaded and yet pursues all their posterity. So that all men "are by nature the children of wrath," [Ephesians 2:3] obnoxious to condemnation, and to temporal as well as to eternal death; they are also devoid of that original righteousness and holiness. [Romans 6:12, 18, 19] With these evils they would remain oppressed forever, unless they were liberated by Christ Jesus; to whom be glory forever.[48]

". . . in his *lapsed and sinful state*," Arminius wrote elsewhere, "man is not capable, of and by himself, either to think, to will, or to do that which is really good; but it is necessary for him to be regenerated and renewed in his intellect, affections or will, and in all his powers, by God in Christ through the Holy Spirit, that he may be qualified rightly to understand, esteem, consider, will, and perform whatever is truly good. When he is made a partaker of this regeneration or renovation, I consider that, since he is delivered from sin, he is capable of thinking, willing and doing that which is good, but yet *not without the continued aids of Divine Grace*."[49]

Both Wesley and Arminius affirmed the substitutionary, penal satisfaction doctrine of the atoning death of Christ. In commenting on Romans 3:25, Wesley wrote that Christ's propitiatory sacrifice was made to

---

[48] Arminius, *Public Disputations*, VII, xv-xvi, in *Ibid.*, 1:485-6.

[49] Arminius, *Declaration of Sentiments*, III, in *Ibid.*, 1:252-3.

> appease an offended God. But if, as some teach, God never was offended, there was no need of this propitiation. And if so, Christ died in vain. *To declare his righteousness*—To demonstrate not only his clemency, but his justice: even that vindictive justice, whose essential character and principal office is, to punish sin. . . .[50]

In explaining the priestly office of Christ, Arminius wrote that by it God exercised both His love for men and His love for justice,

> united to which is a hatred against sin. It was the will of God that each of these kinds of love should be satisfied. He gave satisfaction to his *love for the creature* who was a sinner, when he gave up his Son who might act the part of Mediator. But he rendered **satisfaction** to *his love for justice and to his hatred against sin*, when he imposed on his Son the office of Mediator by the shedding of his blood and by the suffering of death; [Hebrews 2:10; 5:8, 9] and he was unwilling to admit him as the Intercessor for sinners except when sprinkled with his own blood, in which he might be made [*expiatio*] the **propitiation** for sins. [Hebrews 9:12] . . . In this respect also it may with propriety be said that God rendered satisfaction to himself, and appeased himself in "the Son of his love."[51]

Both Wesley and Arminius affirmed that we are justified by God's crediting the righteousness of Christ to our account as a gift through faith apart from works. Commenting on Romans 5:14, Wesley wrote, ". . . as the sin of Adam, without the sins which we afterward committed, brought us death; so the righteousness of Christ, without the good works which we afterward performed, brings us life. . . ."[52] And Arminius similarly wrote,

---

[50] Wesley, *Explanatory Notes*, p. 370.

[51] Arminius, *Public Disputations*, XIV, xvi, 1:560; italicized emphases original, boldfaced emphases added.

[52] Wesley, *Explanatory Notes*, p. 375.

> I believe that sinners are accounted righteous solely by the obedience of Christ; and that the righteousness of Christ is the only meritorious cause on account of which God pardons the sins of believers and reckons them as righteous as if they had perfectly fulfilled the law. But since God imputes the righteousness of Christ to none except believers, I conclude that, in this sense, it may be well and properly said, *To a man who believes, Faith is imputed for righteousness through grace*, because God hath set forth his Son, Jesus Christ, to be a propitiation, a throne of grace, [or mercy seat] through faith in his blood.[53]

In each of these points, Moral Government Theology stands in stark contradiction not only to Arminius and Wesley but also to the great creeds and doctrinal statements of every branch of Protestantism[54] and, most important, to Scripture. If Wesley, the great champion of Christian tolerance and catholicity, could treat rejection of the doctrines of original sin and moral inability alone as sufficient to define one as "a Heathen still," surely MGT, which makes not only this grave error but also many others graver still, must be classified not as a form of Christianity but as heathenism masquerading as Christianity.

---

[53] Arminius, *Declaration of Sentiments*, IX, 1:264.

[54] I have cited these at great length in point-by-point opposition to the primary tenets of MGT in chapter 3.

Chapter Two

The Omniscience of God: Biblical Doctrine and Answers to Objections

"A saying of Chrysostom's," wrote John Calvin, "has always pleased me very much, that the foundation of our philosophy is humility.[1] But that of Augustine pleases me even more: 'When a certain rhetorician was asked what was the chief rule in eloquence, he replied, "Delivery"; what was the second rule, "Delivery"; what was the third rule, "Delivery"; so if you ask me concerning the precepts of the Christian religion, first, second, third, and always I would answer, "Humility."'"[2]

It is not by accident that the first of the beatitudes in the Sermon on the Mount was "Blessed are the poor in spirit, for theirs is the Kingdom of Heaven" (Matt. 5:3). Poverty of spirit—humility—is the *sine qua non* of the Christian life, the indispensable first step of faith. Without it, there is no repentance, there is no teachableness, there is no awe or wonder or praise of the glory and greatness and majesty of God. It is also not by accident that humility stands at the height of the Christian life, at the pinnacle of awareness of God. For it is, so to speak, the well from which springs the fountain of doxology:

[1] Chrysostom, *De profectu evangelii* 2 (MPG 51. 312).

[2] John Calvin, *Institutes*, II. ii. 11; citing Augustine, *Letters* cxiii. 3. 22 (MPL 33. 442).

> Oh, the depth of the riches both of the wisdom and knowledge of God! How unsearchable are His judgments and His ways past finding out!
>
> "For who has known the mind of the LORD?
> Or who has become His counselor?"
> "Or who has first given to Him
> And it shall be repaid to him?"
>
> For of Him and through Him and to Him are all things, to whom be glory forever. Amen (Rom. 11:33-36).

It is a tragic fact, a fact that fills me with sadness—a fact that almost makes me despair in sheer amazement—that anyone who calls himself a Christian, who names Christ as Lord, who professes fidelity to the Holy Scriptures, who claims to be a child of God and to worship the sovereign LORD of the universe, should deny to that LORD the perfection of infinite knowledge. And why? Because he cannot humbly admit his own creatureliness and the devastation brought on him by sin—the sin he inherited from his father Adam just as surely as he inherited the nobility of bearing the image of God as a free agent, a nobility he is quick and jealous to defend, at the same time that he repudiates the corruption he is quick and jealous to deny.

The testimony of the Church through the ages, grounded in Scripture, is so united, so strong, and so fervent on the infinity, the perfection, and the immutability of God in all His attributes, including His absolute omniscience, including His complete foreknowledge of all things, that it is astounding, even irritating, that some professing Christians should dispute it. Why this battle even needs to be fought today escapes me, until I remember that every generation of Christians, in grappling with the spirit of its own age—that spirit of the world that is ever changing yet ever the same—every generation of believers must make the great creeds its own, must discover anew for itself the depth of their wisdom and their fidelity to Scripture.

Debasing God to Exalt Man

The spirit of our age, Francis Schaeffer warns in *The Great Evangelical Disaster*, is "the idea of 'freedom'—not just freedom as an abstract ideal, or in the sense of being free from injustice, but *freedom in an absolute sense. . . .*" It is "autonomous Man setting himself up as God, in defiance of the knowledge and the moral and spiritual truth which God has given."[3] Slightly over a century ago, it required the atheist William Ernest Henley, in the poem *Invictus*—"Unconquered"—to pen the words, "I am the master of my fate; I am the captain of my soul."[4] Today those lines could be the rallying cry of a growing and insidious movement among professing Christians, a movement calling itself "Moral Government Theology" and sometimes—wrongly, as we shall see—equated with classical Arminianism, that, to assert the autonomy of man, blasphemously denies the perfection of God.

But these people are no more the masters of their fate than was Henley. When he penned the famous poem, Henley lay in a hospital bed on the verge of death, having lost one leg to infection and in danger of losing the other, depending for his very survival on the loving and brilliant care of the Christian doctor Joseph Lister, whose advances in antiseptic medicine—founded on the discoveries of another Christian doctor, Louis Pasteur—saved his leg and his life.

Just so it is only by the patient, providential grace of God that those who deny His perfections live from day to day. While they vainly declare the absolute freedom of their wills as the boundary of His knowledge, it remains true from moment to moment that it is in Him, and in Him alone, that they live and move and have their being, "since He gives to all life, breath, and *all things*" (Acts 17:28, 25)—all things

---

[3] Francis A. Schaeffer, *The Great Evangelical Disaster* (Westchester, IL: Crossway Books, 1984), pp. 20, 22.

[4] William Ernest Henley, *Invictus* ("Unconquered").

including even the "free wills" by which they so futilely declare their own autonomy, demonstrating that to be unconquered by God is merely to be not yet surrendered to Him.

Unwilling to admit the bondage of their own wills to their corrupt nature—which they also disavow—they insist, "The power to the contrary is essential to free agency—A free moral agent may always act contrary to any influence, not destructive to his freedom, that may be brought to bear upon him."[5] For them, "Voluntary responsible action involves the possibility of non-compliance or of contrary choice—the freedom of uncertainty. Virtuous action must be voluntary action. If no contrary choice, then no virtuous choice. . . ."[6] And just as surely as they are unwilling to admit the bondage of their wills to their corrupt nature, they also are unwilling to admit the certainty of their choices in the foreknowledge of God, all because of their devotion to "freedom," by which they really mean nothing short of *autonomy*, the absolute independence of the moral agent from any limiting factor. In the words of their chief systematizer, Gordon Olson, the "future choices of moral beings, when acting freely in their moral agency, have not been brought into existence as yet and thus are not fixities or objects of possible knowledge." Indeed, "This applies to actions of the Godhead as well as to the self-caused actions of men."[7]

Their stubborn commitment to the fantasy of "the power of contrary choice" leads them, then, to deny not only God's foreknowledge of *their* acts but even of *His* acts—in outright contradiction of His own self-revelation:

> Remember this, and show yourselves men;
> Recall to mind, O you transgressors.
> Remember the former things of old,
> For I am God, and there is no other;

---

[5] Olson, *Sharing*, p. W-Me-IV-7.
[6] Olson, *Truth*, p. T-V-1.
[7] *Ibid.*, p. T-III-13.

> I am God, and there is none like Me,
> Declaring the end from the beginning,
> And from ancient times things that are not yet done,
> Saying, "My counsel shall stand,
> And I will do all My pleasure."
> Calling a bird of prey from the east,
> The man who executes My counsel, from a far country.
> Indeed I have spoken it;
> I will also bring it to pass.
> I have purposed it;
> I will also do it (Is. 46:8-11).

Can this god they worship be the God who "predestined us to adoption as sons by Jesus Christ to Himself, according to the good pleasure of His will, to the praise of the glory of His grace, by which He made us accepted in the Beloved," who "works *all things* according to the counsel of His will" (Eph. 1:5-6, 11)?

But just as they do not stop at denying to God perfect foreknowledge of the free choices of men, but insist on denying to Him the foreknowledge of His own free choices, so also they do not hesitate to descend to the depths of blasphemy by fastening on Him the same definition of freedom they clutch to themselves, namely, "the power of contrary choice."[8] On the supposition that "Our analysis of our own abilities of personality . . . will aid greatly in understanding the nature of the great Divine Personalities,"[9] and having determined that our freedom consists in "the power of contrary choice," that "Personalities have the mysterious ability to originate action and are not controlled by some causation

[8] *Ibid.*, p. T-III-22.

[9] *Ibid.*, p. T-III-8. (The unusual application to God of the word *personalities* [rather than the orthodox *persons*] appears to be more than a simple idiosyncracy with Olson, who, like many Pelagians before him, faltered at the doctrine of the Trinity, calling God "a trinity of personal spiritual beings [*sic*]" whose oneness was "of purpose and activity" [p. T-III-1], explaining "that the oneness that exists among the Members of the Godhead is a moral or voluntary oneness of character and relationship" [p. T-III-3].)

acting upon the will"[10]—not even some causation internal to the willing agent, as we shall see—they infer that the members of the blessed Trinity "have the mysterious ability of voluntary moral choice, or self-direction. They have chosen to use Their immeasurable energies in a constructive or benevolent manner, the results being called 'the wisdom of God.'"[11] Just as, for man, "Holiness and sin are free voluntary acts of will or states of mind, and, although strongly influenced, *are not caused by any internal force of nature*, tendency, or instinct, nor by persuasion from external sources,"[12] so also for God, "Moral attributes involve the element of choice, or have a voluntary causation to them. They are not natural attributes in that they are not endowments of God's existence, but are moral in the sense that they are the result of a disposition of will. They exist *because each Member of the Godhead perpetually chooses that they should be so*. Moral character must be an active something. It cannot be a static fixity of some sort back of the will, causing its actions."[13] And so they reason from what man has become by the Fall to what God is, rather than from what God is to what man was meant to be. They create God in their own image, in direct contempt of God's warning, "To whom will you liken Me, and make Me equal and compare Me, that we should be alike?" (Is. 46:5).

I digress somewhat here from the focus of this chapter—on the omniscience of God—not by accident but with a purpose: to demonstrate the tremendous stakes involved in accepting the primary principle of the opponents of God's perfect and complete foreknowledge. The starting point of their whole philosophy is their belief that free moral agency necessarily involves "the power of contrary choice."[14] From this

---

[10] *Ibid.*, p. T-III-8.

[11] *Ibid.*, p. T-III-9.

[12] *Ibid.*, p. T-V-I, emphasis added.

[13] *Ibid.*, p. T-III-23, emphasis added.

[14] See the extensive and carefully discriminating discussion of this in Charles Hodge, *Systematic Theology*, 2:278-309.

follows their insistence that what is freely chosen cannot be certain but must be absolutely contingent—caused neither by any internal fixity of nature (and hence they deny original sin and moral inability[15]—two other central and classical doc-

---

[15] Olson insists that man has "ability of intellect," "ability of emotion," and "ability of free will or self-determination" (Olson, *Truth*, p. T-IV-2); that "Holiness and sin are free voluntary acts of will or states of mind, and, although strongly influenced, are not caused by any internal force of nature, tendency, or instinct" (Olson, *Truth*, p. T-V-1); that "Sin is not . . . an abstract thing which invades and lodges somewhere in our personalities, but is rather an orderly sequence of wrong choices and conduct" (Olson, *Truth*, p. T-V-3); that "Depravity strongly influences, but does not compel, toward wrong action. We choose to follow our inclinations when we sin" (Olson, *Truth*, p. T-VI-5); that "Moral depravity . . . is always a voluntary development which results from the wrong choices of our wills" (Olson, *Truth*, p. T-VI-6); that "Moral depravity . . . is always a voluntary development. . . . The universality of sin in the world is not to be accounted for, therefore, by some fixed causation in our personality inherited by birth" (Olson, *Sharing*, pp. W-Me-IV-4-5); that "So-called inability is a question of 'will not' rather than 'cannot' obey God's reasonable rquirements" (Olson, *Sharing*, p. W-Me-VIII-6). (Other proponents of Moral Government Theology similarly deny original sin and human inability. See George Otis Jr., *The God They Never Knew*, pp. 63, 59; Winkie Pratney, *Youth Aflame!*, 1983, pp. 83, 93, 76, 94; Theodore W. Elliott, *Born Sinful? Original Sin* [Springfield, IL: One Way Fellowship, n.d.], *passim.*) Since Olson explicitly denies that man inherits sin or guilt from Adam (*i.e.*, he denies the doctrine of original sin—the imputation of Adam's sin and guilt to his posterity), it should come as no surprise that he also denies the imputation of Christ's righteousness to believers, finding the cause of salvation not in Christ's atoning death but in the believer's self-reformation: "Romans 5:12-19 does not establish the dogma of the literal imputation of Adam's sin to all his posterity, but merely affirms in a parallelism that just as Adam's sin was the occasion, not cause, of the voluntary disobedience of all men, so Christ is the occasion, not cause, of the salvation offered to all men" (Olson, *Truth*, p. T-VI-8). Hence it is clear that by starting with the definition of freedom as the "power of contrary choice" he is forced ultimately to deny nearly the whole defining body of Christian faith: original sin, fallen man's moral inability, the imputation of Christ's righteousness in justification (parallel to the imputation of Adam's sin in condemnation), and the moral and intellectual infinity, perfection, and immutability of God. But pursuing *all* of these elements of Olson's system would take us too far afield from the topic of this essay.

trines of orthodox Christianity) nor by any external compulsion or necessity; and if it cannot be certain, it cannot be foreknown. From this also follows their insistence that if God is a free moral agent, His free choices too cannot be certain but must be absolutely contingent; and if not certain, then not foreknown. And from this it necessarily follows that God's future moral character is neither certain nor foreknown but contingent; *i.e.*, that God's continued goodness is not guaranteed. And so along with God's intellectual perfection and immutability, we must deny also His moral perfection and immutability. To put it simply, we have no ground whatever for assurance that God will not decide tomorrow to become the devil.

That this is the logical and unavoidable implication of their philosophy is clear. No doubt they disavow this implication with all sincerity—or at least some of them do. But sincerity, good and commendable as it is, can never substitute for sound thinking in testing all things, holding fast to that which is good (1 Thes. 5:21).

They might, to substantiate their denial, point to a curious passage in Olson's writings, in which he appears to put an internal limit on God's free agency (an "internal force of nature," he might have called it, did he not explicitly deny that "free voluntary acts of will or states of mind" could be "caused by any internal force of nature"[16]): "God's nature and moral character imposes limitations. God is able to do whatever He wills (except with moral beings), but His will is limited to doing those things which are in harmony with His wise and holy and perfect character. God cannot do things contrary to Himself. This is not a defect in Divine omnipotence but a perfection of the Divine Being."[17]

But we find no consolation here, no assurance that God will continue good tomorrow. For God's character, says

---

[16] Olson, *Truth*, p. T-V-1.
[17] *Ibid.*, p. T-III-22.

Olson, like all moral character, "must be an active something. It cannot be a static fixity of some sort back of the will, causing its actions. Moral character is dynamic; it is the whole personality in action; it is what we are doing with our endowments or abilities of personality and the moral understanding which we possess."[18] God's character, in other words, is determined moment by moment by God's choices; it is "the result of a disposition of will" and because "each Member of the Godhead perpetually chooses that [it] should be so."[19] If it is true that Olson believes that God's "will is limited to doing those things which are in harmony with His wise and holy and perfect character,"[20] it is also true that Olson believes that God's character "cannot be a static fixity of some sort back of the will, causing its actions" but "is the whole personality in action; it is what [God is] doing with [His] endowments or abilities of personality and the moral understanding which [He] possess[es]."[21] "Moral attributes," Olson insists, "involve the element of choice, or have a voluntary causation to them. They are not natural attributes in that they are not endowments of God's existence, but are moral in the sense that they are the result of a disposition of will. They exist because each Member of the Godhead perpetually chooses that they should be so."[22]

So while God's "will is limited to doing those things which are in harmony with His wise and holy and perfect character," this can only be so as long as His character remains wise and holy and perfect, and nothing can guarantee that it will do so forever, for character by definition "cannot be a static fixity," must "involve the element of choice, or have a voluntary causation" to it—must, in short, be "the result of a disposition of will." As Olson puts it, "The will determines the

[18] *Ibid.*, p. T-III-23.
[19] *Ibid.*
[20] *Ibid.*, p. T-III-22.
[21] *Ibid.*, p. T-III-23.
[22] *Ibid.*

nature or character, rather than the nature the will."[23] Should it ever occur that God chooses to make His character other than wise and holy and perfect—and no "internal force of nature" can prevent His doing so—then of course that wise and holy and perfect character will no longer limit what He wills.[24]

The god of Moral Government Theology is a sorry substitute for the God of Scripture—the God infinite, eternal, and immutable in His being, wisdom, power, justice, holiness, goodness, and truth, as the *Westminster Shorter Catechism* puts it. The god of Moral Government Theology is neither infinite, eternal, and immutable in his wisdom nor infinite, eternal, and immutable in his justice, holiness, goodness, and truth. Dare we hope that one attribute is left to him—his power? No. That, too, bows before the awesome freedom of man. Olson hinted at it in a parenthetical phrase in his statement of the limits on his god's will, cited above: "God is able to do whatever He wills *(except with moral beings)*, but His will is limited to doing those things which are in harmony with His wise and holy and perfect character."[25] He makes it explicit when he writes,

> Man as an endowed moral being has been given the ability to *limit the omnipotence of God* in his sphere of life. Mankind by their rebellion against God and their obstinacy in refusing the mercy and forgiveness through the atoning death of Christ have imposed very great limitations upon God's will and happiness. . . . God in creating moral creatures with *the power of contrary choice* made this a possibility.[26]

---

[23] Olson, *Holiness and Sin*, p. 24.

[24] The inherent inconsistency in Olson's system is evident here. On one page he makes the will dependent on the character; on the next page he makes the character dependent on the will. Such elementary deficiencies in logic and analysis are abundant in Olson's writings.

[25] Olson, *Truth*, p. T-III-22, emphasis added.

[26] *Ibid.*, emphases added.

So there you have it: (1) the god of Moral Government Theology: finite and imperfect and changeable in his power, wisdom, justice, holiness, goodness, and truth; (2) the man of Moral Government Theology: perfectly free and able to limit God's power, will, and knowledge. And from these necessarily flows (3) the gospel of Moral Government Theology: that "the atoning death of Christ," as Olson deigns to call it—nay, even Christ Himself—"is the occasion, not cause, of the salvation offered to all men."[27] The "consequences of right and wrong moral action" in Moral Government Theology ". . . are based *solely upon personal merit or demerit* as known only to God" and "are and will be in exact accord or in proportion to merit and demerit."[28]

It is, as I have said, tragic and heartbreaking that the doctrine of God's omniscience should need defense not against self-avowed pagans but against those who profess the Christian faith, for (1) it is the doctrine of Scripture, the rule of the Christian faith; (2) it is the doctrine of the Church through the ages, a trustworthy guide to the meaning of Scripture, a guide from which one should depart only for the most compelling reasons—namely, an insuperable argument from Scripture, which the opponents of omniscience have never provided; and (3) opposition to it arises chiefly from sinful pride, while the first of the virtues—on which hang all others, including the understanding of Scripture—is humility.

First, second, third, and always, humility. That is

---

[27] *Ibid.*, p. T-VI-8. Compare Elliott, *Born Sinful?*, p. 16: "All that [Romans 5:12-19] is showing is that Adam was the occasion of sin and Jesus is the occasion of salvation. Without a being with the ability to choose between holiness and sin, there could be no virtue or blame in that being. He would be under the law of cause and effect. The ability to choose holiness or sin was the occasion or opportunity for sin to enter the world, through Adam . . . . Christ is also the occasion of salvation. Without Him, salvation is impossible. He is the opportunity or circumstance where by [*sic*] man can be saved. This is not to say that all are saved because of Him, just as all are not lost because of Adam, only that the opportunity is present."

[28] Olson, *Truth*, pp. T-IV-10-11, emphasis added.

Augustine's answer to the siren song of freedom falsely so called. Humility! Humility! Humility!

Let us see, then, the omniscience of the true God of Scripture, and learn the lesson Job learned:

> I know that You can do everything, and that no purpose of Yours can be withheld from You. You asked, "Who is this who hides counsel without knowledge?" Therefore I have uttered what I did not understand, things too wonderful for me, which I did not know. Listen, please, and let me speak; You said, "I will question you, and you shall answer Me." I have heard of You by the hearing of the ear, but now my eye sees You. Therefore I abhor myself, and repent in dust and ashes (Job 42:2-4).

God's Omniscience is Revealed in Scripture

The omniscience of God is revealed in Scripture in a variety of ways, from explicit statements to implicit assumptions to propositions whose logical implications are unavoidable.

• *God knows all things.* Explicitly stated, "God . . . knows all things" (1 John 3:20). Not just some things; not all things except those things that "have not been brought into existence as yet and thus are not fixities or objects of possible knowledge"—Olson's description of the future choices of free moral agents acting in their moral agency.[29] *God knows all things.*[30]

---

[29] *Ibid.*, p. T-III-13.

[30] It might be objected, "If God knows all things, then does God know things that are false? Does He know that 2+2=5?" The objection fails to recognize that knowing is always true. What God *knows*, God knows truly. (And, because God is perfect, what God thinks, God also thinks truly. But while man *knows* only truly, he may *think* falsely—and even think he *knows* what he falsely *thinks*, while in fact he does not know it.) Therefore, since it is not true that 2+2=5, God cannot know that 2+2=5; but since it is false that 2+2=5, God knows (truly) that it is false that 2+2=5.

Notice the absurdity of Olson's stated reason for excluding from things knowable the future choices of free moral agents. Why are they not "objects of possible knowledge"? Because they "have not been brought into existence as yet." This of course cuts too broad a swath through God's foreknowledge even for Olson. Consider. Through Joseph, God foretold seven years of plenty and seven years of famine for Egypt (Gen. 41:26-27, 29-30). Yet the years of feast and famine had "not been brought into existence as yet" and thus—if we are to accept Olson's logic—"were not fixities or objects of possible knowledge." Was God merely guessing, then, that they *might* occur? Did He exercise some superhuman facility in meteorological analysis that afforded an exceptionally high degree of reliability to His prediction—so long as it stopped short of true knowledge? If it is truly just the fact that the feast and famine were "not brought into existence as yet" that made them not "objects of possible knowledge," then this conclusion is inescapable.

It might, however, be replied, "But the years of feast and famine were not the result of the free choices of free moral agents acting freely in their moral agency. Look! The text itself says, 'God has shown Pharaoh what *He* [God] is about to do,' and '. . . the dream was repeated to Pharaoh twice because the thing is established by God, and God will shortly bring it to pass' (Gen. 41:28, 32)." Very well. But the years of feast and famine did not yet exist. If, then, God foreknew them—truly foreknew them, so that they were certain—then non-existence does not disqualify something as an object of possible knowledge for God.

"But God foreknew the coming years of feast and famine precisely because He had predetermined that they would come to pass. That is what made them certain." I will not argue with the truth of the claim; it is only what the Scriptures everywhere declare and what the Church in all ages has taught. But I must point out that it is in stark contradiction to this philosophy's own view of free moral agency and of God Himself. For according to Olson, "free voluntary acts of will or states of mind . . . *are not caused by any internal force of nature*."[31] In short, no choice of any free moral agent at one time can *force* that agent to make some particular choice at a later time. If God is a free moral agent, then His choice at one time to send the years of feast and famine must have been free, "not caused by any internal force of nature." But if He is a free moral agent, then His choice at a later time to fulfill His earlier choice to send the years of feast and famine must have been free, "not caused by any internal force of nature." His earlier choice—which prompted the prophetic dreams and their interpretation—cannot have compelled His later choice to fulfill the prophecy in history.

"But God's first choice—to give the prophecy—defined His will and character in a particular way, to which His later choice was bound to comply." The response will not suffice. For according to Olson, "Voluntary responsible action involves the possibility of non-compliance or of contrary choice—the freedom of uncertainty. Virtuous action must be voluntary action. If no contrary choice, then no virtuous choice. . . ."[32] Was God's choice to fulfill the prophecy voluntary? Then it cannot have been "caused by any internal force of nature"[33]—including any hypothetical binding effect of His earlier free choice on His character. And indeed, we should know, on the grounds of Olson's philosophy, that God's earlier will-defined character could not bind His later choice, since "The will determines the nature or character, rather than the nature the will."[34] Whatever definition His first choice gave to His character, His second choice remained completely undetermined; it remained to be seen, by observing that absolutely unconstrained second choice, whether His character would remain the same or change. For, after all,

[31] Olson, *Truth*, p. T-V-I, emphasis added.

[32] *Ibid.*

[33] *Ibid.*

[34] Olson, *Holiness and Sin*, p. 24.

"Moral attributes [including faithfulness] involve the element of choice, or have a voluntary causation to them. They are not natural attributes in that they are not endowments of God's existence, but are moral in the sense that they are the result of a disposition of will. They exist because each Member of the Godhead perpetually chooses that they should be so."[35] And if one or more of the Members of the Godhead stopped choosing that they should be so? Nothing—*nothing*—in the nature of God or free agency, according to this philosophy, provides any reason to believe they cannot or will not.

Was God's choice to fulfill the prophecy—that is, to keep His promise—virtuous? Then He must have had, at the moment He made the second choice, the "power of contrary choice," for "If no contrary choice, then no virtuous choice." So long as this philosophy remains wedded to the notion of freedom as autonomy, as the "power of contrary choice," it must arrive at one of two conclusions. Either (1) God's promises do not bind Him regarding the future, and therefore we have no ground for assurance that He will keep them—even those on which we rely absolutely for our own salvation; or (2) there is nothing virtuous or praiseworthy in God's keeping His promises, and we only pretend to worship when we sing, "Great is Thy faithfulness! Great is Thy faithfulness! Morning by morning new mercies I see. All I have needed, Thy hand hath provided. Great is Thy faithfulness, Lord, unto me!"

"Then perhaps it really was simply that God, with His perfect knowledge of the material world as it then existed, could extrapolate with perfect reliability from the weather at one point what would be the weather for the next fourteen years. Perhaps He really was merely predicting cause-and-effect physical relationships, something that even we can do, though to a lesser extent and with less accuracy and reliabil-

[35] Olson, *Truth*, p. T-III-23.

ity." Aside from the fact that this expressly denies what the text says about the years of feast and famine—that *God* would "shortly bring [them] to pass" (Gen. 41:32; *cf.* v. 28)—this, too, leaves us in an inextricable dilemma. If God's power was sufficient to change the cause-and-effect course of nature so as to make the prediction false, then the truth of the prediction hung always and only on whether God would choose to use His power that way; and as we have seen, nothing about that choice could have been determined by any internal force, such as God's prior self-defining decisions. In that case, God really did not foreknow the coming of the feast and famine. But if God's power was not sufficient to change the cause-and-effect course of nature so as to make the prediction false, then we have abandoned all pretense at belief in an omnipotent God, and we are talking instead about a god no greater than the gods of Olympus—lesser, even, for at least they could interfere in the weather! Thus the god of Moral Government Theology finds his omnipotence limited not only by the "free will" of man the moral agent, but also by the material cause-and-effect relationships of creation. Not sovereignty alone but providence also disappears, and we are left deists.

No, the truth of the matter is simply what Scripture says: "God . . . knows all things" (1 John 3:20)—including things not brought into existence as yet, whose present non-existence does *not* exclude them from the category of "objects of possible knowledge." The God who "calls those things which do not exist as though they did" (Rom. 4:17) "knows *all* things."

• *Nothing can be hidden from God.* The corollary of "God knows all things" is that nothing is or can be hidden from God. This is precisely what we are taught by Scripture. "If I say, 'Surely the darkness shall fall on me,' even the night shall be light about me; indeed the darkness shall not hide from You, but the night shines as the day; the darkness and the light are both alike to You" (Ps. 139:11-12). ". . . there is no creature hidden from His sight, but all things are naked and open to the eyes of Him to whom we must give account" (Heb. 4:13). It is tempting to respond, "Yes, all things are naked and open to God. But things that do not yet exist are not among 'all things.'" But that is merely to attach to the infinite and eternal God limitations that properly apply only to finite and temporal creatures. It is to ignore the testimony of Romans 4:17, just cited: God "calls those things which do not exist as though they did." In knowing all things, God knows things presently existing as things presently (in relation to temporal things) existing, and things not yet existing as things not yet (in relation to temporal things) existing; but He knows them both with equal certitude, they are equally certain in His sight.[36]

• *God's understanding is infinite.* To say that God knows all things and that nothing can be hid from God is equivalent to saying that God's knowledge is limitless, unbounded. And that is precisely what Scripture says of it: "Great is our Lord, and mighty in power; His understanding is infinite" (Ps. 147:5). What is infinite is endless, unbounded, without limits. And what is infinite cannot grow, for if it did it would be greater after its growth than before, which would prove that it was not infinite before.

If God's understanding is infinite, then His foreknowledge must be absolute and complete, *i.e.*, there must be nothing about the future that He does not know, for if there were, then when it became an accomplished fact, He would know it, and His knowledge would grow—*i.e.*, His understanding would not have been infinite in the first place. Thus, if the

---

[36] To say this is not to suggest that God is time bound. Present and future apply only to temporal beings, not to the eternal God. When we say that God knows "things future as things future," we mean that He knows things that are, in relation to temporal things, future, as things that are, in relation to temporal beings, future. But in relation to Himself, all things that are, in relation to temporal beings, past, present, and future are equally known without reference to any temporality attaching to Himself, which is why He calls "those things which do not exist as though they did."

"future choices of moral beings, when acting freely in their moral agency, have not been brought into existence as yet and thus are not fixities or objects of possible knowledge,"[37] then God's understanding is not infinite, and the Scripture is wrong. May it never be!

• *God's knowledge can never increase.* Because God's understanding is infinite, His knowledge can never increase: "Who has directed the Spirit of the LORD, Or as His counselor has taught Him? With whom did He take counsel, and who instructed Him, And taught Him in the path of justice? Who taught Him knowledge, And showed Him the way of understanding?" (Is. 40:13-14); "For who has known the mind of the Lord? Or who has become His counselor?" (Rom. 11:34). If God were to learn something new every time a moral agent made a free choice, then every moral agent would have "taught Him knowledge, and showed Him the way of understanding," every man would have "become His counselor."

• *God's knowledge is absolutely comprehensive.* This is simply the same as saying that God knows all things. But Scripture teaches us this in various ways and in relation to various categories of things to be known.

• *God's knowledge is comprehensive in space.* The "eyes of the LORD run to and fro throughout the whole earth" (2 Chr. 16:9). Does this imply that He learns new things as He searches about? That would contradict what we have already seen of His infinite knowledge and of His never learning anything new. No, the point of the metaphor—and metaphor it must be, since God does not have literal eyes with feet on which they run to and fro throughout the whole earth—the point must be that no where in all creation escapes His constant observation. His omnipresence makes the comprehensivity of His knowledge in relation to space inescapable, as the psalmist discovered: "O LORD, You have searched me and known me. You know my sitting down and my rising up; You un-

---

[37]Olson, *Truth*, p. T-III-13.

derstand my thought afar off. . . . Such knowledge is too wonderful for me; it is high, I cannot attain it. Where can I go from Your Spirit? Or where can I flee from Your presence? If I ascend into heaven, You are there; if I make my bed in hell, behold, You are there. If I take the wings of the morning, and dwell in the uttermost parts of the sea, even there Your hand shall lead me, and Your right hand shall hold me" (Ps. 139:1-2, 6-10).

• *God's knowledge is comprehensive in time.* "My frame was not hidden from You, when I was made in secret, and skillfully wrought in the lowest parts of the earth. Your eyes saw my substance, being yet unformed. And *in Your book they all were written, the days fashioned for me, when as yet there were none of them*" (Ps. 139:15-16). God's absolute and unerring knowledge of the future sets Him apart absolutely from all temporally finite things, so that He can challenge the idols and those who worship them by comparing their ignorance of the future with His knowledge of it. "'Present your case,' says the LORD. 'Bring forth your strong reasons,' says the King of Jacob. 'Let them bring forth and show us what will happen; let them show the former things what they were, that we may consider them, and know the latter end of them; or declare to us things to come. Show the things that are to come hereafter, that we may know that you are gods. . . . Indeed you are nothing, and your work is nothing; he who chooses you is an abomination.'" But not so God: "'*I* have raised up one from the north, and he shall come; from the rising of the sun he shall call on My name; and he shall come against princes as though mortar, as the potter treads clay. Who has declared from the beginning, that we may know? And former times, that we may say, "He is righteous"?'" (Is. 41:21-23a, 25-26).

Jesus made His ability to predict the future with absolute certainty an evidence of His deity when He said, "Now I tell you before it comes, that when it does come to pass, you may believe that I am" (John 13:19).[38] Christ's foreknowledge of the one who would betray Him would not be evidence of His deity if it did not differ qualitatively from man's predictive abilities; not a mere probability—as might be attributed to shrewd psychological insight—but a certainty of prediction is in mind here. Indeed, Christ could not even have foreknown that Judas would betray Him, on the supposition that freedom always presupposes the power of contrary choice. If the choices of free moral agents are not limited by any internal causal factor such as character, as Moral Government Theology teaches, then Judas's choice could not have been foreknown merely on the basis of his character, since "The will determines the nature or character, rather than the nature the will."[39]

Olson's inconsistency is clear when he seeks to preserve Judas's free agency in betraying Christ despite Christ's foreknowledge of it by writing, "It does not appear that the treachery of Judas was specifically prophesied in the Old Testament, nor that the Lord Jesus expected his apostasy *until He perceived its development in his mind*. If our Lord expected it all the time, why was He 'troubled in spirit' or heartstricken at its development (Jn. 13:21)? It is obviously presented as a tragic surprise."[40] If free agency presupposes the power of contrary choice, and if "The will determines the character or nature rather than the nature the will," then right up to the moment when Judas's betrayal passed from a future contingency to a past event Judas could always have chosen otherwise.

The very principle on which Olson bases his denial of

---

[38] Note that the word *He* at the close of the verse is not in the Greek text. The final Greek clause, *ego eimi*, asserts Christ's eternal existence. Compare John 8:58; Exodus 3:14; Isaiah 43:10. Thus Christ presents His absolute foreknowledge of the one who would betray Him as evidence of His deity.

[39] Olson, *Holiness and Sin*, p. 24.

[40] Olson, *Truth*, p. T-III-20, emphasis added.

God's foreknowledge of the free choices of moral agents—the power of contrary choice—destroys his own explanation of how Judas's betrayal could be both free and foreknown. But not only Judas's choice. Much more is at stake. Olson writes, "Many future choices, actions, and mass reactions of men appear to be known to God beforehand and form the basis for many detailed plans of events that God purposes to bring to pass in making reconciliation for all men possible in His government of world affairs."[41] Among these are "The rejection and putting to death of Christ, the Messiah and Saviour, whom God purposed to send into the world because of sin." How could God foreknow this sinful—*i.e.*, moral and therefore free and uncertain—choice in which all men joined? Olson explains:

> The Lord Jesus would come as "the light of the world" (Jn. 8:12), as "a high priest, holy, innocent, undefiled, separated from sinners" (He. 7:26), into a world that "loved the darkness rather than the light" (Jn. 3:19), energized by and under the dominion of "the evil one" (Ep. 2:2; 1 Jn. 5:19), "the father of lies" (Jn. 8:44). The Saviour's total witness "that its deeds are evil" (Jn. 7:7) would call for such a revolutionary change that God the Father expected a total rejection by the masses and made His plans accordingly.[42]

Consider what Olson's absolute commitment to the "power of contrary choice" as the ground of all moral agency does to this argument. He says that Jesus came as "the light of the world," "a high priest, holy, innocent, undefiled, separated from sinners," apparently as if this indicated something about Jesus' moral character. But since "The will determines the character or nature rather than the nature the will," there was never any assurance that Jesus would remain so throughout His sojourn on earth—or even that He would remain so

[41] *Ibid.*, p. T-III-13.
[42] *Ibid.*, pp. T-III-13-14.

through all the millennia prior to His incarnation. He says that Jesus came into a world that "loved the darkness rather than the light," apparently as if this indicated something about the character of the world—and of the people who constituted it. But since "The will determines the character or nature rather than the nature the will," nothing could ensure beforehand that, long before God's plan to send a Savior was ever enacted, this world, including all the people in it, would not stop loving the darkness and start loving the light instead, making the Savior's visit unnecessary and giving God another opportunity to make "new decisions," to "change His mind when certain reactions took place." He says that the world lies "under the dominion of 'the evil one.'" But if this means anything at all, then it means that somehow the "dominion of the evil one" determined the character and choices of the world that made the world's rejection of Christ inevitable. Yet it is precisely such a dominion over the choices of free moral agents, a dominion that makes "the power of contrary choice" empty, that Olson denies both to God and to the internal character of free moral agents themselves. Thus in Olson's system, the devil has the power to do what God cannot do: control the choices of free moral agents! He calls the devil "the evil one" and "the father of lies." But is the devil a moral agent? If so, then he, too, always has "the power of contrary choice," and so nothing could ensure that his dominion would not turn into "the dominion of the righteous one," in which case he would not have incited men to reject the Savior (the Savior they no longer needed, by the way). He writes that on the basis of His understanding of the character of this world—this world that loved darkness rather than light and was energized by and under the dominion of the evil one—the Father "expected a total rejection by the masses and made His plans accordingly." But if the devil is a free moral agent, and if people are free moral agents, and if the power of contrary choice is essential to free moral agency, then there was no ground for the Father to expect their total rejection of the Messiah, and there were no grounds for His planning accordingly.

Precisely such analysis destroys Olson's explanation of every instance of God's foreknowledge of any element of the future that is morally significant, whether we have in mind the choices and acts of individuals or of nations or of the whole human race. God had no more ground for expecting Israel to "rebel and require judgments" to bring it "back to repentance and forgiveness"[43] than He had to expect the world to reject the Messiah. Olson's pessimistic eschatology, too, collapses under the weight of this analysis, for while Olson writes, "Because of God's knowledge of man's extreme unwillingness to receive the truth and repent of sin, God knows that the world will never be converted to Christ but will become more and more determined in pursuit of self gratification,"[44] his commitment to the principle of "the power of contrary choice" makes meaningless his assertion of "man's extreme unwillingness to receive the truth and repent of sin," for at any given moment any and every man might choose—since "The will determines the character or nature rather than the nature the will"—to be willing to receive the truth and repent of sin instead. This argument does not force on Olson a view he never held, it merely takes him at his word. "Moral character," he insists,

> is a voluntary state of activity or conduct that takes place in the experiences and consciousnesses of moral beings. Moral character is moral action or personal action. . . . Moral character is not something back of the will causing action, not a fixed entity lodging somewhere in our being, but the action of the will itself. . . . Moral character is what we are doing with our endowments of personality and the moral light that we possess—our thoughts, attitudes, actions. . . . Moral action is, therefore, free or self-originated

---

[43] *Ibid.*, p. T-III-14.
[44] *Ibid.*

> action, and moral character is a description of what habitual actions are taking place.[45]

Even when Olson finds himself compelled to acknowledge the existence of some defining character underlying the will, he can never admit that this character ultimately obligates the will: "Depravity strongly influences, but does not compel, toward wrong action."[46] And always the internal contradiction in his view emerges again, as when he writes, shortly after the last proposition, one that presupposes the opposite relation between depravity and choice: "Moral depravity . . . is always a voluntary development which results from the wrong choices of our wills."[47] Which is it? Does depravity define choice, or does choice define depravity? Olson cannot have it both ways. The effect cannot precede its cause, nor the cause follow its effect. And the underpinning presupposition of his whole system—that the power of contrary choice is essential to free agency—determines that it is ultimately choice that defines depravity, not vice versa.

Indeed, it is precisely on this point—that man's absolute ability to repent is finally unrestricted by any internal or external cause—that Olson is most insistent.

> It is *not* that man is unable to repent or respond to God's mercy that requires any special means of reconciliation. . . . Scripture speaks of the will or heart as the source of all moral actions. . . . Scripture addresses man as possessing the ability and responsibility of self-decision. . . . Scripture commands "that all everywhere should repent" and nowhere states that man is unable to do so. . . . Therefore, although man's unwillingness to repent and be conquered by the loving mercy of God is a monumental problem that *God has not been able to solve*, man's natural ability is not for he painfully possesses this.[48]

[45] *Ibid.*, p. T-V-1-2.
[46] *Ibid.*, p. T-VI-5.
[47] *Ibid.*, p. T-VI-6.
[48] *Ibid.*, emphases added.

> Is man able to repent?
>
> In our discussion of the nature of sin we saw that sin is always a voluntary state or attitude of will in supremely preferring our own happiness rather than God's and our fellowmen's. While depravity strongly influences the will and has been developed to its present strength by our own actions, nevertheless we are the author [*sic*] of our own actions. So-called inability is a question of "will not" rather than "cannot" obey God's reasonable requirements.[49]

To those who deny His absolute foreknowledge, God gives this exhortation: "Remember this, and show yourselves men; recall to mind, O you transgressors. Remember the former things of old, for I am God, and there is no other; I am God, and there is none like Me, declaring the end from the beginning, and from ancient times things that are not yet done, saying, 'My counsel shall stand, and I will do all My pleasure'" (Is. 46:8-10). And lest they respond, "But that only shows that God knows what *He* has determined to do in the future," we must remind them to be consistent: if God is a free agent, and the power of contrary choice is necessary to free agency, then no earlier determination on God's part can bind Him for the future, since "The will determines the nature or character, rather than the nature the will."[50] Furthermore, according to Olson, "God is represented in the Bible as making new decisions, as pondering situations and as making up His mind in conformity thereto, and as changing His mind when certain reactions took place."[51] "Many Bible passages, when taken in their natural meaning, appear to indicate that God does not have absolute foreknowledge over all His own future actions, nor over all those of His moral creatures."[52] Yet Scripture says, "Known to God from eternity are all His works" (Acts 15:18).

---

[49] *Ibid.*, p. T-X-9.
[50] Olson, *Holiness and Sin*, p. 24.
[51] Olson, *Truth*, p. T-III-13.
[52] *Ibid.*, p. T-III-18.

When God said to Israel through Isaiah, "I am God, and there is none like Me, declaring the end from the beginning, and from ancient times things that are not yet done, saying, 'My counsel shall stand, and I will do all My pleasure,'" it was to assure Israel that His determination to judge that kingdom for its idolatry would never change (Is. 46:5-7). The method he had determined for executing that judgment was to bring Cyrus and his armies against Israel (Is. 46:11; 44:28). But if the power of contrary choice is necessary to free agency, then God could not be certain that Israel would not repent, *en masse*, of its idolatry before the judgment came, and if He persisted in punishing Israel after its repentance, the punishment would, from Olson's viewpoint, be unjust. Neither could God be certain that Cyrus would not choose not to attack Israel, or that Cyrus's soldiers would not choose to be cowards or mutineers who rebelled against Cyrus's orders and refused to attack Israel. Yet God pronounces His intention to punish Israel, using Cyrus as His tool, with absolute certainty, as a demonstration that He is God.

• *God's Knowledge is Comprehensive in Scope, Including All Things from the Greatest to the Least.* God "counts the number of the stars; He calls them all by name" (Ps. 147:4). Yet He sees our ways and counts all our steps (Job 31:4). He knows our sitting down and our rising up; He understands our thoughts from afar; He comprehends our path and our lying down; indeed, said David, "there is not a word on my tongue, but behold, O Lord, You know it altogether" (Ps. 139:2-4), and even "the very hairs of your head are all numbered" (Matt. 10:30).

This is what Job learned when God laid bare Job's ignorance and revealed His own omniscience. "By what way is light diffused, or the east wind scattered over the earth? . . . Do you know the ordinances of the heavens? . . . Who has put wisdom in the mind? Or who has given understanding to the heart? Who can number the clouds by wisdom? . . . Do you know the time when the wild mountain goats bear young?

Or can you mark when the deer gives birth? Can you number the months that they fulfill? Or do you know the time when they bear young? . . . Does the hawk fly by your wisdom, and spread its wings toward the south? . . . Shall the one who contends with the Almighty correct Him?" (Job 38:24, 33, 36-37; 39:1-2, 26; 40:2).

At this rebuke Job withered. "Behold, I am vile," he said; "what shall I answer You? I lay my hand over my mouth. Once I have spoken, but I will not answer; yes, twice, but I will proceed no further" (Job 40:4-5). But God wasn't finished with Job. He pointed to the heart of Job's faulty understanding of God when He demanded, "Would you indeed annul My judgment? Would you condemn Me that you may be justified?" (Job 40:8). Similarly, the heart of Moral Government Theology's resistance to God's foreknowledge is its belief that there can be no moral responsibility—and hence no judgment—where there is no "power of contrary choice": "The ability of personality to originate and be responsible for all actions is the foundation of moral responsibility and accountability."[53] And if to affirm the power of contrary choice we must deny that God is infinite, eternal, and immutable in His knowledge and in His moral excellenc— if we must make God's understanding finite and His justice, holiness, goodness, and truth tenuous—then so be it. Why, Olson even goes so far as to write, "Moral government involves an amazing study in contrasts as the great God is represented as appealing in humility to the heart of man, so profoundly small in his limitations, to conform to His wise and holy ways in blessed fellowship. . . ."[54]

When God asks, "Would you condemn Me that you may be justified?" Moral Government Theology responds, Yes. Not man, but God, is humbled in this system. Man is exalted. His "freedom" is seen as the limiting factor on both

---

[53] *Ibid.*

[54] *Ibid.*, p. T-IV-6.

God's knowledge and God's omnipotence. No philosophy more opposite that of the Scriptures can be imagined.

• *God's knowledge comprehends not only things actual but also things contingent—not only what actually has come to pass, or will come to pass, but whatever could have come to pass, or could yet come to pass, on any supposition.* Thus we read of a time when David benefitted from God's knowledge of contingencies: "'O LORD God of Israel,'" David prayed,

> "Your servant has certainly heard that Saul seeks to come to Keilah to destroy the city for my sake. Will the men of Keilah deliver me into his hand? Will Saul come down, as Your servant has heard? O LORD God of Israel, I pray, tell Your servant." And the LORD said, "He will come down." Then David said, "Will the men of Keilah deliver me and my men into the hand of Saul?" And the LORD said, "They will deliver you." So David and his men, about six hundred, arose and departed from Keilah and went wherever they could go. Then it was told Saul that David had escaped from Keilah; so he halted the expedition (1 Sam. 23:10-13).

God stated with certainty what would have ensued if His people had repented of their sins, although in fact they did not: "Oh, that My people would listen to Me, that Israel would walk in My ways! I would soon subdue their enemies, and turn My hand against their adversaries. The haters of the LORD would pretend submission to Him, but their fate would endure forever. He would have fed them also with the finest of wheat; and with honey from the rock I would have satisfied you" (Ps. 81:13-16). His declaration depends not only on knowing what He Himself would have done but also on knowing what other free moral agents would have done—those who would have pretended submission to Him.

God told Zedekiah precisely and certainly what would happen depending on either of two choices Zedekiah could make: "Thus says the LORD, the God of hosts, the God of Israel: 'If you surely surrender to the king of Babylon's princes, then your soul shall live; this city shall not be burned with fire, and you and your house shall live. But if you do not surrender to the king of Babylon's princes, then this city shall be given into the hand of the Chaldeans; they shall burn it with fire, and you shall not escape from their hand'" (Jer. 38:17-18; *cf.* 19-23).

Jesus combined knowledge both of the contingent (but non-actual) past and of the certain future when He pronounced,

> Woe to you, Chorazin! Woe to you, Bethsaida! For if the mighty works which were done in you had been done in Tyre and Sidon, they would have repented long ago in sackcloth and ashes. But I say to you, it will be more tolerable for Tyre and Sidon in the day of judgment than for you. And you, Capernaum, who are exalted to heaven, will be brought down to Hades; for if the mighty works which were done in you had been done in Sodom, it would have remained until this day. But I say to you that it shall be more tolerable for the land of Sodom in the day of judgment than for you (Matt. 11:20-24).

And notice this about Jesus' foreknowledge of the judgment to come on Chorazin and Bethsaida and Capernaum: it would come because of their rejection of the truth attested by His mighty works. If they were to be judged for that rejection, it must be voluntary—it could not be among those rare occurrences in which God sets aside the normal moral freedom and accountability of moral agents, placing the will "temporarily under a law of cause and effect."[55] But if they repented of that rejection—which Olson (and with him all others who assert that the power of contrary choice, unhindered by any force external or internal, including the agent's own character, is essential to free agency) must believe they could have done at any moment in their histories—then they

[55] *Ibid.*, p. T-III-15.

would no longer merit the punishment, according to Moral Government Theology, which teaches that repentance alone, without the payment of a propitiating or appeasing penalty to the demands of justice, brings forgiveness.[56] And nothing in their character, no internal force whatever—let alone any external force—could necessitate their persisting in that rejection, according to this theory. So if Jesus was right in predicting with absolute certainty that God would so judge Chorazin and Bethsaida and Capernaum, then God had determined to do so regardless of any moral desert on the part of the cities—in which case God is unjust. But then how could Jesus have known with such certainty that God would indeed judge these cities so? After all, God, as a free agent whose will defined His character rather than vice versa, could at any time change His mind.

But Scripture will have none of such nonsense. Despite all appeals to anthropomorphic language depicting changes

[56] "A voluntary disposition of mercy and forgiveness prevails equally among all the Members of the Godhead. The Godhead are without personal vindictiveness. The problems of forgiveness are not personal but governmental. God does not require an exact payment for sin to satisfy retributive justice, but only requires that an atonement shall satisfy public justice and all the problems of a full and free reconciliation in His government of moral beings" (Olson, *Truth*, p. T-VII-4). This denial of any demand for the satisfaction of retributive (or vindictive) justice in God leads Olson to deny that Christ's atoning death was the true payment of a penalty to satisfy the justice of God: "The sacrifice of Christ is not the payment of a debt, nor is it a complete satisfaction of justice for sin. It is a Divinely-appointed [*sic*] condition which precedes the forgiveness of sin, just as the death of a lamb or a goat in the Mosaic economy. Christ's sufferings took the place of a penalty, so that His sufferings have the same effect in reconciling God to man, and procuring the forgiveness of sin, that the sinner's endurance of the punishment due to his sins would have had. The sufferings of Christ were not a substituted penalty, but a substitute for a penalty" (Olson, "Historical Opinions as to the Nature of Christ's Atoning Death," 3, in *Truth*, following p. T-VII-10). The atonement of Christ "[r]endered satisfaction to public justice (a demonstration before all that rebellion against authority will be punished), as distinguished from retributive or vindictive justice" (Olson, *Truth*, p. T-VIII-4).

in God's plans—language rooted in human perspective—the testimony of Scripture is that God is perfect in His infinite, eternal, and immutable attributes, and that these attributes, both intellectual and moral, ensure that whatever He predicts will come to pass, whatever He promises He will fulfill. "God is not a man, that He should lie, nor a son of man, that He should repent. Has He said, and will He not do? Or has He spoken, and will He not make it good?" (Num. 23:19). It is in Jesus Christ, who is the Alpha and Omega, the Beginning and the End, the First and the Last, the One who is and who was and who is to come, the same yesterday, today, and forever, that "all the promises of God . . . are Yes, and in Him Amen, to the glory of God through us" (2 Cor. 1:20; *cf.* Rev. 1:8, 11; Heb. 13:8). All our security, all our assurance of His protection, rests on His unchanging nature, character, and will: "For I am the LORD, I do not change; therefore you are not consumed, O sons of Jacob" (Mal. 3:6). In this God alone do we dare trust.

> For when God made a promise to Abraham, because He could swear by no one greater, He swore by Himself, saying, "Surely blessing I will bless you, and multiplying I will multiply you." And so, after he had patiently endured, he obtained the promise. For men indeed swear by the greater, and an oath for confirmation is for them an end of all dispute. Thus God, determining to show more abundantly to the heirs of promise the *immutability of His counsel*,[57] confirmed it by an oath, that by two immutable things, in which it is impossible for God to lie, we might have strong consolation, who have fled for refuge to lay hold of the hope set before us. This hope we have as an anchor of the soul, both sure and steadfast, and which enters the Presence behind the veil, where the forerunner has entered for us, even Jesus (Heb. 6:13-20).

---

[57] *New King James Version* margin, "unchangeableness of His purpose."

God's Omniscience is the Doctrine of the Church through the Ages

In light of the compelling testimony of Scripture, the Church of Christ with united voice through the centuries has proclaimed the absolute omniscience—including the foreknowledge—of God, echoing the words of John, that "God . . . knows all things" (1 John 3:20). This is not to say that no professing Christian has ever denied this truth; it is Scripture, not Church history, that is inerrant and infallible. But it is to say that the unity on this doctrine is so overwhelming as to imply that anyone who departs from it does so in contempt, not respect, for the voice of the Bride.

A thorough survey of the whole of Church history on this point is neither necessary nor, in this context, possible. It should be sufficient to show that none of the chief streams of Protestant theology—Lutheran, Calvinist, Wesleyan, or Arminian—countenances any denial of God's perfect and complete foreknowledge. Indeed, as we shall see, most of the creeds go far beyond simply affirming God's complete foreknowledge, affirming also His election and predestination. My citation of such passages as do so here is not intended to persuade anyone of predestination but merely to suggest that, if those who wrote the creeds believed in that, they cannot have failed to believe also in foreknowledge.

Thus, the Lutheran *Formula of Concord* (1576) says, "[T]he foreknowledge of God is nothing else than this, that God knows all things before they come to pass. . . . This foreknowledge of God extends both to good and evil men; but nevertheless it is not the cause of evil, nor is it the cause of sin, impelling man to crime" (Article XI, Affirmative, sects. ii-iii).

The *French Confession of Faith*, prepared by John Calvin and his pupil De Chandieu, revised and approved by a synod at Paris in 1559, says,

We believe that [God] not only created all things, but that He governs and directs them, disposing and ordaining by his sovereign will all that happens in the world; not that he is the author of evil, or that the guilt of it can be imputed to him, as his will is the sovereign and infallible rule of all right and justice; but he hath wonderful means of making use of devils and sinners that he can turn to good the evil which they do, and of which they are guilty. And thus, confessing that the providence of God orders all things, we humbly bow before the secrets which are hidden to us, without questioning what is above our understanding; but rather making use of what is revealed to us in Holy Scripture for our peace and safety, inasmuch as God, who has all things in subjection to him, watches over us with a Father's care, so that not a hair of our heads shall fall without his will (Article VIII).

The *Belgic Confession* (1561) says,

We believe that the same God, after he had created all things, did not forsake them, or give them up to fortune or chance, but that he rules and governs them, according to his holy will, so that nothing happens in this world without his appointment; nevertheless, God neither is the author of, nor can be charged with, the sins which are committed. For his power and goodness are so great and incomprehensible, that he orders and executes his work in the most excellent and just manner even when the devil and wicked men act unjustly. And as to what he doth surpassing human understanding we will not curiously inquire into it further than our capacity will admit of; but with the greatest humility and reverence adore the righteous judgments of God which are hid from us, contenting ourselves that we are disciples of Christ, to learn only those things which he has revealed to us in his Word without transgressing these limits.

This doctrine affords us unspeakable consolation, since we are taught thereby that nothing can befall us by chance, but by the direction of our most gracious and heavenly Father, who watches over us with a paternal care, keeping

> all creatures so under his power that not a hair of our head (for they are all numbered), nor a sparrow, can fall to the ground without the will of our Father, in whom we do entirely trust; being persuaded that he so restrains the devil and all our enemies that, without his will and permission, they cannot hurt us (Article XIII).

The *Thirty-Nine Articles of the Church of England* (English Edition, 1571; American Revision, 1801) says,

> Predestination to Life is the everlasting purpose of God, whereby (before the foundations of the world were laid) he hath constantly decreed by his counsel secret to us, to deliver from curse and damnation those whom he hath chosen in Christ out of mankind, and to bring them by Christ to everlasting salvation, as vessels made to honour. Wherefore, they which be endued with so excellent a benefit of God, be called according to God's purpose by his Spirit working in due season: they through Grace obey the calling: they be justified freely: they be made sons of God by adoption: they be made like the image of his only-begotten Son Jesus Christ: they walk religiously in good works, and at length, by God's mercy, they attain to everlasting felicity.
>
> As the godly consideration of Predestination, and our Election in Christ, is full of sweet, pleasant, and unspeakable comfort to godly persons, and such as feel in themselves the working of the Spirit of Christ, mortifying the works of the flesh, and their earthly members, and drawing up their mind to high and heavenly things, as well because it doth greatly establish and confirm their faith of eternal Salvation to be enjoyed through Christ, as because it doth fervently kindle their love towards God: So, for curious and carnal persons, lacking the Spirit of Christ, to have continually before their eyes the sentence of God's Predestination, is a most dangerous downfall, whereby the Devil doth thrust them either into desperation, or into wretchlessness of most unclean living, no less perilous than desperation (Article XVII).

The *Lambeth Articles* (1595)—a Calvinist appendix to the *Thirty-Nine Articles*, say,

> God from eternity hath predestinated certain men unto life; certain men he hath reprobated. The moving or efficient cause of predestination unto life is not the foresight of faith, or of perseverance, or of good works, or of any thing that is in the person predestinated, but only the good will and pleasure of God. There is a predetermined certain number of the predestinate, which can neither be augmented nor diminished (Articles 1-3).

It is significant that despite the strong words about predestination included in the *Thirty-Nine Articles*, Calvinists in the Church of England thought it necessary to add these articles as an appendix; the *Thirty-Nine Articles*, in other words, cannot simply be written off as Calvinist.

The *Irish Articles of Religion* (1615) say,

> God from all eternity did, by his unchangeable counsel, ordain whatsoever in time should come to pass; yet so, as thereby no violence is offered to the wills of the reasonable creatures, and neither the liberty nor the contingency of the second causes is taken away, but established rather.
>
> By the same counsel God hath predestinated some unto life, and reprobated some unto death: of both which there is a certain number, known only to God, which can neither be increased nor diminished.
>
> Predestination to life is the everlasting purpose of God whereby, before the foundations of the world were laid, he hath constantly decreed in his sacred counsel to deliver from curse and damnation those whom he hath chosen in Christ out of mankind, and to bring them by Christ unto everlasting salvation, as vessels made to honor.
>
> The cause moving God to predestinate unto life is not the foreseeing of faith, or perseverance, or good works, or of any thing which is in the person predestinated, but only the good pleasure of God himself. For all things being ordained for the manifestation of his glory, and his glory be-

ing to appear both in the works of his mercy and of his justice, it seemed good to his heavenly wisdom to choose out a certain number towards whom he would extend his undeserved mercy, leaving the rest to be spectacles of his justice.

Such as are predestinated unto life be called according unto God's purpose (his spirit working in due season), and through grace they obey the calling, they be justified freely; they be made sons of God by adoption; they walk religiously in good works; and at length, by God's mercy, they attain to everlasting felicity. But such as are not predestinated to salvation shall finally be condemned for their sins.

The godlike consideration of predestination and our election in Christ is full of sweet, pleasant, and unspeakable comfort to godly persons, and such as feel in themselves the working of the spirit of Christ, mortifying the works of the flesh and their earthly members, and drawing up their minds to high and heavenly things: as well because it doth greatly confirm and establish their faith of eternal salvation, to be enjoyed through Christ, as because it doth fervently kindle their love towards God; and, on the contrary side, for curious and carnal persons lacking the spirit of Christ to have continually before their eyes the sentence of God's predestination is very dangerous (Articles 11-16).

The *Westminster Confession* says,

God, the great Creator of all things, doth uphold, direct, dispose, and govern all creatures, actions, and things, from the greatest even to the least, by his most wise and holy providence, according to his infallible foreknowledge and the free and immutable counsel of his own will, to the praise of the glory of his wisdom, power, justice, goodness, and mercy. . . . Although in relation to the foreknowledge and decree of God, the first cause all things come to pass immutably and infallibly, yet by the same providence he ordereth them to fall out, according to the nature of second causes, either necessarily, freely, or contingently (Chapter V, Articles i-ii).

The *Confession of the Free-Will Baptists* (1834, 1868), while asserting complete freedom of the human will, yet asserts the absolute foreknowledge of God:

> God exercises a providential care and superintendence over all his creatures, and governs the world in wisdom and mercy, according to the testimony of his Word. God has endowed man with power of free choice, and governs him by moral laws and motives; and this power of free choice is the exact measure of his responsibility. All events are present with God from everlasting to everlasting; but his knowledge of them does not in any sense cause them, nor does he decree all events which he knows will occur (Chapter III).

The *Confession of the Evangelical Free Church of Geneva* (1848) says,

> We believe that the beginning and the end of our salvation, our new birth, faith, sanctification, and perseverance are a gratuitous gift of the divine mercy; the true believer having been elected in Christ before the foundation of the world, according to the foreknowledge of God, the Father, in the sanctification of the Holy Ghost, to obey Jesus Christ and to be bathed in his blood (Article X).

The *Methodist Articles of Religion* (1784) say, "There is but one living and true God, everlasting, without body or parts, of *infinite* power, *wisdom*, and goodness" (Article I).

These are just a few samples of the manners in which the creeds of Protestantism affirm the foreknowledge of God, all the while maintaining that the human will is still free in the sense that it is self-determined and therefore responsible and accountable for all its choices.[58] Because some proponents of

[58] This is to be distinguished from saying that the will determines the self—*i.e.*, from affirming free self-determination. It is precisely the self—the character—that biblical Christianity says no man can freely determine, since moral character is inherited from Adam. While Moral Government Theology affirms that the will defines the character, biblical Christianity affirms that the character defines the will; choice stems from nature, not nature from choice.

Moral Government Theology—and therefore opponents of the foreknowledge of God—represent the issue as a debate between Calvinism and Arminianism or Wesleyanism, it should be helpful also to see how Arminius and Wesley themselves thought about God's foreknowledge.

James Arminius clearly affirmed the absolute omniscience and complete foreknowledge of God as necessitated by God's very nature:

> IMMUTABILITY is a pre-eminent mode of the Essence of God, by which it is void of all change; of being transferred from place to place, because it is itself its own end and good, and because it is immense; of generation and corruption; of alteration; increase and decrease; for the same reason as that by which it is incapable of suffering. (Psalm cii, 27; Mal. iii, 6; James i, 17). Whence likewise, in the Scriptures, INCORRUPTIBILITY is attributed to God.[59]

> God . . . knows all things possible, whether they be in the capability of God or of the creature; in active or passive capability; in the capability of operation, imagination, or enunciation. He knows all things that could have an existence, on laying down any hypothesis. He knows [*alia a se*] other things than himself, those which are necessary and contingent, good and bad, universal and particular, future, present and past, excellent and vile. He knows things substantial and accidental of every kind; the actions and passions, the modes and circumstances of all things; external words and deeds, internal thoughts, deliberations, counsels, and determinations, and the entities of reason, whether complex or simple. All these things, being jointly attributed to the understanding of God, seem to conduce to the conclusion, that God may deservedly be said to know things infinite. (Acts xv, 18; Heb. iv, 13; Matt. xi, 27; Psalm cxlvii, 4; Isai. xli, 22, 23; xliv, 7; Matt. x, 30; Psalm cxxxv; 1 John iii, 20; 1 Sam. xvi, 7; 1 Kings viii, 39; Psalm xciv, 11; Isai. xl, 28; Psalm cxlvii, 5; cxxxix; xciv, 9, 10; x, 13, 14). . . . All the

[59] Arminius, *Public Disputations*, IV, xviii.

things which God knows, He knows neither by intelligible [species] images, nor by similitude, (for it is not necessary for Him to use abstraction and application for the purpose of understanding;) but He knows them by his own essence, and by this alone, with the exception of evil things which He knows indirectly by the opposite good things; as, through means of the habitude, privation is discovered. THEREFORE, 1. God knows himself *entirely* and *adequately*. . . . 2. He knows himself primarily; . . . 3. [*Intelligere Dei*] The act of understanding in God is his own being and essence. . . . The mode by which God understands, is not that which is successive, and which is either through composition or division, or through [*discursum*] deductive argumentation; but it is simple, and through infinite intuition. (Heb. iv, 13). THEREFORE, 1. God knows all things from eternity; nothing [*de novo*] recently. For this new perfection would add something to His essence by which He understands all things; or his understanding would exceed His essence, if he now understood what he did not formerly understand. But this cannot happen, since he understands all things through his essence. (Acts xv, 18; Ephe. i, 4). 2. He knows all things immeasurably, without the augmentation and decrease of the things known and of the knowledge itself. (Psalm cxlvii, 5). 3. He knows all things immutably, his knowledge not being varied to the infinite changes of the things known. (James i, 17). 4. By a single and [*individuo*] undivided act, not [*distractus*] being diverted towards many things but collected into himself, He knows all things. Yet he does not know them confusedly, or only universally and in general; but also in a distinct and most special manner He knows himself in himself, things in their causes, in themselves, in his own essence, in themselves [*praesenter*] as being present, in their causes antecedently, and in himself most pre-eminently. (Heb. iv, 13; 1 Kings viii, 39; Psalm cxxxix, 16, 17). . . . The understanding of God is certain, and never can be deceived, so that He certainly and infallibly sees even future contingencies, whether He sees them in their causes or in themselves. (1 Sam. xxiii, 11, 12; Matt. xi, 21). But, this certainty rests upon the infinite essence of God, by which in a manner the most present

> He understands all things. . . . The understanding of God [*causatur*] is derived from no external cause, not even from an object; though if there should not afterwards be an object, [*non sit de eo futura,*] there would not likewise be the understanding of God about it. (Isai. xl, 13, 14; Rom. xi, 33, 34).[60]

Wesley, too, affirmed God's perfect foreknowledge, while leaving room for human free agency. Commenting on John 6:64 ("For Jesus had known from the beginning who they were that believed not, and who would betray him"), he wrote, "Therefore it is plain, God does foresee future contingencies:—

> 'But his foreknowledge causes not the fault,
> Which had no less proved certain unforeknown.'"[61]

Failed Objection Based on Confusion Over Moral Freedom

This strong testimony of the Church affirms what we saw before from Scripture: that God's omniscience is truly all-comprehensive, limited not by time or space or human freedom. Yet, as Charles Hodge noted in his *Systematic Theology*, there have been a few voices—a very few, compared with the vast body of the faithful—who have disagreed.

> The Socinians, however, and some of the Remonstrants,[62] unable to reconcile this foreknowledge with human lib-

[60] *Ibid.*, IV, xxxi-xxxiii, xxxvi-xxxvii.

[61] Wesley, *Explanatory Notes*, p. 232.

[62] Even the *Articuli Arminiani sive Remonstrantia* (*The Five Arminian Articles*; 1610) did not go so far as to deny the foreknowledge of God. And far from their supporting other elements of Moral Government Theology, they actually deny them, affirming instead the unchangeability of God's purposes in Christ (Article I), that the unregenerate man "has not saving grace of himself, nor of the energy of his free will, inasmuch as he, in the state of apostasy and sin, can of and by himself neither think, will, nor do any thing that is truly good (such as saving Faith eminently is); but that it is needful that he be born again of God in Christ, through his Holy Spirit,

> erty, deny that free acts can be foreknown. As the omnipotence of God is his ability to do whatever is possible, so his omniscience is his knowledge of everything knowable. But as free acts are in their nature uncertain, as they may or may not be, they cannot be known before they occur. Such is the argument of Socinus. This whole difficulty arises out of the assumption that contingency is essential to free agency. If an act may be certain as to its occurrence, and yet free as to the mode of its occurrence, the difficulty vanishes. That free acts may be absolutely certain, is plain, because they have in a multitude of cases been predicted. It was certain that the acts of Christ would be holy, yet they were free. The continued holiness of the saints in heaven is certain, and yet they are perfectly free. The foreknowledge of God is inconsistent with a false theory of free agency, but not with the true doctrine on that subject.[63]

We saw above that the root of Gordon Olson's denial of God's foreknowledge was precisely this: that he believed no choice was free that was not absolutely contingent, *i.e.*, that was in any sense certain. For him, "the power of contrary choice" was the defining mark of free agency.

Olson's inability to reconcile free agency with divine foreknowledge rests on a failure to recognize two crucial distinc-

---

and renewed in understanding, inclination, or will, and all his powers, in order that he may rightly understand, think, will, and effect what is truly good" (Article III), and that "this grace of God is the beginning, continuance, and accomplishment of all good, even to this extent, that the regenerate man himself, without prevenient or assisting, awakening, following and co-operative grace, can neither think, will, nor do good, nor withstand any temptations to evil; so that all good deeds or movements, that can be conceived, must be ascribed to the grace of God in Christ" (Article IV). In other words, the Remonstrants believed in original sin, in moral inability, and in the Reformed *ordo salutis* (order of salvation), which puts regeneration before repentance, faith, and conversion in light of the inability of the unregenerate to think or do anything that is truly good, including to have saving faith. All of these truths the proponents of Moral Government Theology deny.

[63] Hodge, *Systematic Theology*, 1:400-401.

tions. The first of these is that between, as Hodge puts it, "liberty of the will" and "liberty of the agent":

> The usage . . . which makes these expressions synonymous is liable to the following objections: (1.) Predicating liberty of the will is apt to lead to our conceiving of the will as separated from the agent; as a distinct self-acting power in the soul. Or, if this extreme be avoided, which is not always the case, the will is regarded as too much detached from the other faculties of the soul, and as out of sympathy with it in its varying states. The will is only the soul willing. The soul is of course a unit. A self-determination is a determination of the will, and whatever leads to a self-decision leads to a decision of the will. (2.) A second objection to confounding these expressions is, that they are not really equivalent. The man may be free, when his will is in bondage. It is a correct and established usage of language, expressive of a real fact of consciousness, to speak of an enslaved will in a free agent. This is not a mere metaphor, but a philosophical truth. He that commits sin is the servant of sin. [Romans 6:16] Long-continued mental or bodily habits may bring the will into bondage, while the man continues a free agent. A man who has been for years a miser, has his will in a state of slavery, yet the man is perfectly free. He is self-controlled, self-determined. His avarice is himself. It is his own darling, cherished feeling. (3.) There is no use to have two expressions for the same thing; the one appropriate, the other ambiguous. What we really mean is, that the agent is free. That is the only point to which any interest is attached. The man is the responsible subject. If he be free so as to be justly accountable for his character and conduct, it matters not what are the laws which determine the operations of his reason, conscience, or will; or whether liberty can be predicated of either of those faculties separately considered. We maintain that the man is free; but we deny that the will is free in the sense of being independent of reason, conscience, and feeling. In other words, a man cannot be independent of himself, or any one of his faculties independent of all the rest.[64]

[64] *Ibid.*, 2:290-291.

The second crucial distinction Hodge makes is that between liberty and ability.

> The usage which attaches the same meaning to these terms is very ancient. Augustine denied free will to man since the fall. Pelagius affirmed freedom of will to be essential to our nature. The former intended simply to deny to fallen man the power to turn himself unto God. The latter defined liberty to be the ability at any moment to determine himself either for good or evil. The controversy between Luther and Erasmus was really about ability, nominally it was about free-will. Luther's book is entitled "De Servo Arbitrio" [Of the Bondage of the Will], that of Erasmus, "De Libero Arbitrio" [Of the Freedom of the Will]. This usage pervades all the symbols of the Reformation, and was followed by the theologians of the sixteenth century. They all ascribe free agency to man in the true sense of the words, but deny to him freedom of will. To a great extent this confusion is still kept up. Many of the prevalent definitions of liberty are definitions of ability; and much that is commonly advanced to prove the liberty of the will, is really intended, and is of force only as in support of the doctrine of ability. . . . Augustine, and after him most Augustinians distinguished, (1.) The liberty of man before the fall, which was an ability either to sin or not to sin. (2.) The state of man since the fall, when he has liberty to sin, but not to good. (3.) The state of man in heaven when he has liberty to good, but not to evil. This last is the highest form of liberty, a *felix necessitas boni*. This is the liberty which belongs to God. In the popular mind perhaps the common idea of liberty is, the power to decide for good or evil, sin or holiness. This idea pervades more or less all the disquisitions in favour of the liberty of indifference, or of power to the contrary.[65]

Recognizing these two distinctions—between liberty of the will and liberty of the agent, and between liberty and

---

[65] *Ibid.*, 2:291-292.

ability—permits us to understand how a free agent can have a will that is in bondage, *i.e.*, a will that is unable to choose certain things. The phrase *liberty of the agent* means that the agent—the acting person—is not forced by anyone or anything outside himself to choose and to do as he does. He is at liberty respecting external causes; he is responsible for his choices, and he alone. But the phrase *liberty of the will* means that the will is not forced by anything outside *itself*—whether internal or external to the agent—to choose as it does. But if the will is bound by no force outside itself, whether internal or external to the agent whose the will is, then the will is utterly arbitrary and capricious. No will of a moral agent, therefore, is truly free, for the will of every moral agent is directed by that agent's moral and intellectual character. The will may be free in respect of forces external to the agent, but in respect of forces internal to the agent, the will is bound; it cannot make decisions other than as the agent's understanding and moral commitment lead it.

This is true of God and man alike. God is "of purer eyes than to behold evil, and cannot look on wickedness"—that is, cannot look on it with pleasure (Hab. 1:13); His will is bound from delighting in wickedness. Because truth is of the very essence of God, God "cannot lie" (Tit. 1:2); it is "impossible for God to lie" (Heb. 6:18); His will is bound from lying. "God is light and in Him is no darkness at all" (1 John 1:5); His will is bound from all evil. God neither knows nor can be known—not in the mere sense of intellectual acknowledgement or acquaintance, but in that deeper sense of covenantal relationship and union—by anyone who does not love, "for God is love" (1 John 4:8); His will is bound from joining in covenantal union with the wicked. It is precisely because God is righteous—*i.e.*, just—that He *could not* simply leave sin unpunished and declare innocent those who were guilty of sin, precisely because of this that He, if He were going to acquit anyone, had to provide "the gift of righteousness" by the imputation of Christ's righteousness "resulting in justification of life" so that "by one Man's obedience many will be made righteous" (Rom. 5:17-19), so that Paul could write,

> But now the righteousness of God apart from the law is revealed, being witnessed by the Law and the Prophets, even the righteousness of God, through faith in Jesus Christ, to all and on all who believe. For there is no difference; for all have sinned and fall short of the glory of God, being justified freely by His grace through the redemption that is in Christ Jesus, whom God set forth as a propitiation by His blood, through faith, to demonstrate His righteousness, because in His forbearance God had passed over the sins that were previously committed, to demonstrate at the present time His righteousness, that He might be just and the justifier of the one who has faith in Jesus (Rom. 3:21-26).

His will is bound from leaving sin unpunished.

In all of these things, God the agent is absolutely free; nothing external to Him binds Him in any way. But God's *will* is bound, bound by God's character. And it is the immutable righteousness, justice, and faithfulness of God that is the ground of the believer's confidence in prayer when he conforms his prayers to the character of God, as Abraham did when he prayed for Sodom, "Far be it from You to do such a thing as this, to slay the righteous with the wicked, so that the righteous should be as the wicked; far be it from You! Shall not the Judge of all the earth do right?" (Gen. 18:25). God is not able to will anything contrary to His own moral nature or character; His will is not free, although He Himself is free.

So also man. All men, prior to regeneration, "both Jews and Greeks . . . are all under sin" (Rom. 3:9), *i.e.,* are enslaved to it in their own natures, and that is why "There is none righteous, no, not one; there is none who understands; there is none who seeks after God. They have all turned aside; they have together become unprofitable; there is none who does good, no, not one" (Rom. 3:10-12). On the contrary, all are "dead in trespasses and sins . . . the sons of disobedience . . . by nature children of wrath" (Eph. 2:1-3), their choices ruled by "the futility of their mind, having their understanding darkened, being alienated from the life of God, because of the ignorance that is in them because of the blindness of their heart; who, being past feeling, have given themselves over to lewdness, to work all uncleanness with greediness," dominated entirely by "the old man which grows corrupt according to the deceitful lusts" (Eph. 4:17-19, 22). This is why Paul says that, so long as they remain outside of Christ, they are "slaves of sin" (Rom. 6:6, 17, 20), under its dominion (Rom. 6:14), slaves of disobedience (Rom. 6:16), "free in regard to righteousness" (Rom. 6:20)—*i.e.,* not ruled by righteousness but ruled by sin.

Are they free in regard to things external to themselves? Yes. They and they alone make their choices. But are they free in regard to something internal to themselves—to their own moral character? No. They are slaves of sin, sons of disobedience, dead in trespasses and sin, futile in thought, dark in understanding, alienated from the life of God, ignorant, blind in heart, and insensate (Eph. 4:17-19). Thus for every unregenerate man, while he himself is free—nothing outside him forces him to choose as he does—his will is bound by his moral nature or character; it is unable to choose contrary to that nature; it lacks precisely what Olson believes is the essence of freedom, "the power of contrary choice." His will is not free, although he himself is free.

This is why repentance, faith, and conversion are not, and cannot be, the work of unregenerate man. Regeneration must come first, for a bad tree cannot bear good fruit (Matt. 7:18); the tree must be made new, transformed from a bad tree to a good tree, before it can bear good fruit. The man dead in trespasses and sins must be made alive; the son of disobedience must be made a son of obedience; the child of wrath must be made a child of peace; the futile mind must be made effectual; the dark understanding must be enlightened; ignorance must be replaced by knowledge; the blind heart must be made to see; the insensate, seared conscience must be made sensate and tender. None of these transformations can be made by the unregenerate man, but all must be made in order for repentance, faith, and conversion to occur. All are what is meant by regeneration, the new birth, adoption as sons to God, being united with Christ. "Therefore, if anyone is in Christ, he is a new creation; old things have passed away; behold, all things have become new" (2 Cor. 5:17). In the moment that we die to the old man, we live to the new, and "if we have been united together in the likeness of His death, certainly we also shall be in the likeness of His resurrection, knowing this, that our old man was crucified with Him, that the body of sin might be done away with, that we should no longer be slaves of sin. For he who has died has been freed from sin" (Rom. 6:5-7). All these things are done to him, not by him, as indicated in the passive verbs Paul uses: ". . . if we *have been united* together in the likeness of His death, certainly we also shall be in the likeness of His resurrection"; "our old man *was crucified* with Him, that the body of sin *might be done away with*, that we should no longer be slaves of sin. For he who has died *has been freed* from sin. . . . And having *been set free* from sin, you became slaves of righteousness" (Rom. 6:5-7, 18).

The blessed goal toward which every regenerate man is moving, by the grace and faithfulness of God, is glorification, when the last bit of the "old man" will have been erased from his constitution, and he will be undividedly good, perfectly conformed to the image of Jesus Christ (Rom. 8:29-30). From that time on, his free agency will be usable only for good. Having put off corruption and put on incorruption; having put off mortality and put on immortality, he will be forever free from the sting of sin, the victory over sin at last won (1 Cor. 15:50-57). Although he may not know now what he will be, he does know that when Christ is revealed, he will be like Him (1 John 3:2).

The solution to the whole problem of Moral Government Theology—to its denial of God's foreknowledge and moral immutability, to its denial of original sin and depravity, to its denial of the substitutionary, satisfactory atonement, to its teaching that Christ is only the *occasion* of salvation and not its cause, while it assigns to the individual man the cause of salvation—is to pull up its root in the misunderstanding of free agency, its confusion of liberty of the will with liberty of the agent, and of liberty with ability. Toward that end we can pray that God will graciously enable its adherents to attend carefully to, and to understand, this explanation by Charles Hodge:

> It is admitted by this class of writers [namely, those who insist that free agency equals freedom of the will], and, indeed, by the whole Christian world, that men since the fall have not power to make themselves holy; much less to effect this transformation by a volition. It is admitted that saints in glory are infallibly determined by their character to holiness, yet fallen men and saints are admitted to be free. Ability may be lost, yet liberty remain. The former is lost since the fall. Restored by grace, as they say, it is to be again lost in that liberty to good which is identical with necessity. If liberty and ability are thus distinct, why should they be confounded? We are conscious of liberty. We know ourselves to be free in all our volitions. They reveal themselves to our inmost consciousness as acts of self-determination. We cannot disown them, or escape responsibility on account of them, even if we try; and yet no man is conscious of ability to change his own heart. Free agency belongs to God, to angels, to saints in glory, to fallen men, and to Satan; and it is the same in all. Yet in the strictest sense of the words, God cannot do evil; neither can Satan recover, by a volition, his lost inheritance of holiness. It is a great evil thus to confound things essentially distinct. It produces endless confusion. Augustine says, man is not free since the fall, because he cannot but sin; saints are free because they cannot sin. Inability in the one case destroys freedom; inability in the other is the perfection of free-

dom! Necessity is the very opposite of liberty, and yet they are said to be identical. One man in asserting the freedom of the will, means to assert free agency, while he denies ability; another means by it full ability. It is certainly important that the same words should not be used to express antagonistic ideas.

Confusion of thought and language, however, is not the principal evil which arises from making liberty and ability identical. It necessarily brings us into conflict with the truth, and with the moral judgments of men. There are three truths of which every man is convinced from the very constitution of his nature. (1.) That he is a free agent. (2.) That none but free agents can be accountable for their character or conduct. (3.) That he does not possess ability to change his moral state by an act of the will. Now, if in order to express the fact of his inability, we say, that he is not a free agent, we contradict his consciousness; or, if he believe what we say, we destroy his sense of responsibility. Or if we tell him that because he is a free agent, he has power to change his heart at will, we again bring ourselves into conflict with his convictions. He knows he is a free agent, and yet he knows that he has not the power to make himself holy. *Free agency is the power to decide according to our character; ability is the power to change our character by a volition.* The former, the Bible and consciousness affirm belongs to man in every condition of his being; the latter, the Bible and consciousness teach with equal explicitness does not belong to fallen man. The two things, therefore, ought not to be confounded.[66]

Hodge goes on to explain another confusion, that between self-determination of the agent and self-determination of the will. By the latter is intended by those who use the phrase the denial"that the will is determined by the antecedent state of the mind, and to affirm that it has a self-determining power, independent of anything preëxisting or coëxisting," *i.e.*, the affirmation

---

[66] *Ibid.*, 2:292-294.

> that as the will has a self-determining power it may decide against all motives internal or external, against all influences divine or human, so that its decisions cannot be rendered inevitable without destroying their liberty. The very essence of liberty, they say, is power to the contrary. In other words, a free act is one performed with the consciousness that under precisely the same circumstances, that is, in the same internal as well as external state of the mind, it might have been the opposite. According to the [Augustinian] doctrine, the *will* is determined; according to the other, it determines itself. In the one case, our acts are or may be inevitably certain and yet be free. In the other, in order to be free, they must be uncertain.[67]

But beyond all the confusion of terms, there remains "a real difference [of understanding] as to the nature of free agency; and that difference concerns this very point: may the acts of free agents be rendered inevitably certain without destroying their liberty?"[68] Hodge then states points about which the two sides in the debate are agreed: (1) "that man is a free agent, in such a sense as to be responsible for his character and acts"; (2) that "the nature of free agency . . . supposes both reason and active power"—*i.e.*, that brutes and maniacs are not free agents; (3) "that in all important cases, men act under the influence of motives"; (4) "that the will is not determined with certainty by *external* motives"; (5) "that the word *will* is to be taken in its proper, restricted sense. The question is not, whether men have power over their affections, their likes and dislikes. No one carries the power of the will so far as to maintain that we can, by a volition, change our feelings. The question concerns our volitions alone. It is the ground or reason of acts of self-determination that is in dispute. And, therefore, it is the will considered as the faculty

[67] *Ibid.*, 2:294, 296.
[68] *Ibid.*, 2:296.

of self-determination, and not as the seat of the affections, that comes into view."[69]

The whole question therefore is, whether, when a man decides to do a certain thing, his will is determined by the previous state of his mind. Or, whether, with precisely the same views and feelings, his decisions may be one way at one time, and another at another. That is, whether the will, or rather the agent, in order to be free, must be undetermined.[70]

Hodge then launches his argument that free agency is consistent with certainty—and therefore with moral inability on the part of unregenerate man, with moral immutability on the part of God, and with God's foreknowledge of man's choices:

> It is certainly a strong argument in favour of that view of free agency, which makes it consistent with certainty, or which supposes that an agent may be determined with inevitable certainty as to his acts, and yet those acts remain free, that it suits all classes or conditions of free agents. To deny free agency to God, would be to deny Him personality and to reduce Him to a mere power or principle. And yet, in all the universe, is there anything so certain as that God will do right? But if it be said that the conditions of existence in an infinite being are so different from what they are in creatures, that it is not fair to argue from the one to the other, we may refer to the case of our blessed Lord. He had a true body and a reasonable soul. He had a human will; a mind regulated by the same laws as those which determine the intellectual and voluntary acts of ordinary men. In his case, however, although there may have been the metaphysical possibility of evil (though even that is a painful hypothesis), still it was more certain that He would be without sin than that the sun or moon should endure. . . . But if it be objected even to this case, that the union of the divine and human natures in the person of

[69] *Ibid.*, 2:297.
[70] *Ibid.*, 2:297-298.

> our Lord places Him in a different category from ourselves, and renders it unfair to assume that what was true in his case must be true in ours; without admitting the force of the objection, we may refer to the condition of the saints in heaven. They, beyond doubt, continue to be free agents; and yet their acts are, and to everlasting will be, determined with absolute and inevitable certainty to be good. Certainty, therefore, must be consistent with free agency. What can any Christian say to this? Does he deny that the saints in glory are free, or does he deny the absolute certainty of their perseverance in holiness? Would his conception of the blessedness of heaven be thereby exalted? Or would it raise his ideas of the dignity of the redeemed to believe it to be uncertain whether they will be sinful or holy? We may, however, come down to our present state of existence. Without assuming anything as to the corruption of our nature, or taking for granted anything which Pelagius would deny, it is a certain fact that all men sin. There has never existed a mere man on the face of the earth who did not sin. When we look on a new-born infant we know that whatever may be uncertain in its future, it is absolutely, inevitably certain that, should it live, it will sin. In every aspect, therefore, in which we can contemplate free agency, whether in God, in the human nature of Christ, in the redeemed in heaven, or in man here on earth, we find that it is compatible with absolute certainty.[71]

If free agency—moral responsibility for our choices—is consistent with the bondage of the will rightly understood—a bondage to the moral character of the agent whose will does the choosing—then it is consistent with certainty. And if it is consistent with certainty, then it is consistent with foreknowledge. No appeal to the free agency of man, therefore, is an adequate ground for denying the absolute foreknowledge of God.[72]

---

[71] *Ibid.*, 2:298-299.

[72] Clark Pinnock offers another argument for the incompatibility of free agency with foreknowledge, a strange and ill-defined notion that what

Conclusion

The foregoing objectively shows both the truth of God's foreknowledge as revealed in Scripture and its compatibility with human free agency and moral responsibility. But what is *objectively* adequate is not always, and for all people, *subjectively* adequate, for various reasons having to do with our own weaknesses in thought and feeling. What, then, can I say to someone who, having read and considered all of the above, still finds himself undecided? I return to the beginning. With Augustine I say, "if you ask me concerning the precepts of the Christian religion, first, second, third, and always I would answer, 'Humility.'"

Stephen Charnock, in his classic work *The Existence and Attributes of God*, put it well:

> But what if the foreknowledge of God, and the liberty of the will, cannot be fully reconciled by man? Shall we therefore deny a perfection in God to support a liberty in ourselves? Shall we rather fasten ignorance upon God, and accuse him of blindness, to maintain our liberty? That God doth foreknow everything, and yet that there is liberty in the rational creature, are both certain; but how fully to reconcile them, may surmount the understanding of man. Some truths the disciples were not capable of bearing in

---

is foreknown somehow cannot be significant: "I found I could not shake off the intuition that such a total omniscience would necessarily mean that everything we will ever choose in the future will have been already spelled out in the divine knowledge register, and consequently the belief that we have truly significant choices to make would seem to be mistaken." (Clark H. Pinnock, "From Augustine to Arminius: A Pilgrimage in Theology," in *The Grace of God, the Will of Man: A Case for Arminianism*, ed. Clark H. Pinnock [Grand Rapids: Zondervan, 1989], p. 25.) Scripture nowhere hints that "truly significant choices" are only those that surprise God. The significance of choices, according to Scripture, arises from whether they are right or wrong, whether they conform to or violate the law of God, whether they glorify Him or rebel against Him, whether they help or hurt our neighbors.

the days of Christ; and several truths our understandings cannot reach as long as the world doth last; yet, in the mean time, we must, on the one hand, take heed of conceiving God ignorant, and on the other hand, of imagining the creature necessitated; the one will render God imperfect, and the other will seem to render him unjust, in punishing man for that sin which he could not avoid, but was brought into by a fatal necessity. God is sufficient to render a reason of his own proceedings, and clear up all at the day of judgment; it is a part of man's curiosity, since the fall, to be prying into God's secrets, things too high for him; whereby he singes his own wings, and confounds his own understanding. It is a cursed affectation that runs in the blood of Adam's posterity, to know as God, though our first father smarted and ruined his posterity in that attempt; the ways and knowledge of God are as much above our thoughts and conceptions as the heavens are above the earth (Isa. lv. 9), and so sublime, that we cannot comprehend them in their true and just greatness; his designs are so mysterious, and the ways of his conduct so profound, that it is not possible to dive into them. The force of our understandings is below his infinite wisdom, and therefore we should adore him with an humble astonishment, and cry out with the apostle, (Rom. xi. 33): "O the depth of the riches of the wisdom and knowledge of God! how unsearchable are his judgments, and his ways past finding out!" Whenever we meet with depths that we cannot fathom, let us remember that he is God, and we his creatures; and not be guilty of so great extravagance, as to think that a subject can pierce into all the secrets of a prince, or a work understand all the operations of the artificer. Let us only resolve not to fasten anything on God that is unworthy of the perfection of his nature, and dishonorable to the glory of his majesty; nor imagine that we can ever step out of the rank of creatures to the glory of the Deity, to understand fully everything in his nature.[73]

[73] Stephen Charnock, *The Existence and Attributes of God*, 2 vols. (Grand Rapids: Baker, [1681] 1979 reprint.), 1:450-451.

Ask yourself three simple questions: Are there things regarding the conduct of foreign and domestic policy about which you expect the President and his advisors to understand more than you do, granted your limited position and access to facts? How much more ought you to expect that there are things about God beyond your understanding? Rather than making the limits of your understanding the limits of God's ability, does it not make better sense to make the greatness of God the limit of your protest?

Indeed, the final resolution to all such problems is not to be found in the intellect. So long as we are determined to understand everything completely, we will be trapped by the inescapable facts of our own sinfulness and creaturehood. The resolution is to be found in the will—a will that needs transforming by the powerful grace of God. It is to be found in repentance. Job's response to God's demonstration of His transcendent power and wisdom must be ours:

> I know that You can do everything, and that no purpose of Yours can be withheld from You. You asked, "Who is this who hides counsel without knowledge?" Therefore I have uttered what I did not understand, things too wonderful for me, which I did not know. Listen, please, and let me speak; You said, "I will question you, and you shall answer Me." I have heard of You by the hearing of the ear, but now my eye sees You. Therefore I abhor myself, and repent in dust and ashes (Job 42:2-6).

Chapter Three

The Heresy of Moral Government Theology

In Ephesians 4:4-6, the Apostle Paul celebrates the unity of the Body of Christ: "There is one body and one Spirit, just as also you were called in one hope of your calling; one Lord, one faith, one baptism, one God and Father of all who is over all and through all and in all." Shortly after that, however, he warns that this unity may be undermined by false doctrines, writing, ". . . we are no longer to be children, tossed here and there by waves, and carried about by every wind of doctrine by the trickery of men, by craftiness in deceitful scheming . . ." (Eph. 4:14).

The unity of the faith is a glorious reality, but it is not all-encompassing. There are some doctrines that simply are outside its bounds, doctrines that strike at the heart of the one faith. These we must beware of and resist by "speaking the truth in love," thus helping all believers "to grow up in all aspects into Him, who is the head, even Christ, from whom the whole body, being fitted and held together by that which every joint supplies, according to the proper working of each individual part, causes the growth of the body for the building up of itself in love" (Eph. 4:15-16).

In the last two decades, a deviant form of doctrine known generally as "Moral Government Theology" has become popular in some evangelical circles.[1] Although most people

[1] Our concern is not to identify those circles in which Moral Government Theology exercises influence, but to define and refute it. We hope

who embrace it are unaware of the extent to which it conflicts with biblical, orthodox, historic Christianity, it is nonetheless a heretical system of theology. As such, it must be confronted by forthright opposition by responsible evangelicals in loving concern for the unity, integrity, and health of the Bride of Christ.

Some proponents of Moral Government Theology claim that it is simply a version of Wesleyan Arminianism—a theological system long recognized as within the bounds of orthodox Christianity. They label opposition to it as based entirely on the controversy between Calvinism and Arminianism. Hence, they reason, such controversy merely divides the Body of Christ over nonessential doctrines and is therefore unhealthy and unscriptural.

This is not so. Moral Government Theology is neither Arminian nor Wesleyan but is completely outside the range of biblical Christianity. The controversy is not between two brands of Christianity but between Christianity and non-Christianity. This is a serious charge, but it is true nonetheless.

We will prove this below in three steps: (1) showing what Moral Government Theology teaches about (a) the foreknowledge and (b) the goodness of God, (c) the nature of fallen man and sin, (d) the atoning death of Christ, and (e) justification; (2) contrasting that teaching at each point with direct citations of Scripture to show that Moral Government Theology is unbiblical; (3) contrasting that teaching at each point with direct citations from historic Protestant creeds and doctrinal standards from each of its main theological traditions—Calvinism, Lutheranism, and Wesleyanism/Arminianism—and from the writings of Arminius and Wesley themselves.

In our conclusion we will call for all Christians to de-

---

and pray that organizations influenced by it in the past will recognize its errors and turn from them without the need for public confrontation. For a partial list of organizations influenced by or committed to Moral Government Theology, see note 2 on p. 16 and the text and note 5 of pp. 18-19.

nounce Moral Government Theology as heresy and for those who have embraced it in the past to renounce it publicly and embrace biblical orthodoxy in its stead.

This chapter, however, is not solely negative. It is also positive. Below we will see the wonderful unity of the major branches of Protestantism on essential elements of the faith. We consider this unity both worth defending and a cause for rejoicing, and invite our brothers and sisters to join us in both the defense and the rejoicing.

Section I: The Heretical System Defined

Summary of the System

Moral Government Theology is heretical in its doctrines at five main points. It denies (1) God's absolute and unchangeable foreknowledge; (2) God's absolute and unchangeable goodness; (3) the biblical doctrine of sin, especially of original sin as constituting both moral corruption and guilt on the part of all Adam's posterity for his sin, and as disabling unregenerate man from any works pleasing to God; (4) the biblical doctrine of the atonement, particularly, that in the atonement Christ, substituting Himself for sinners, paid the penalty for sin and bore the punishment for it, thus satisfying the justice of God; and (5) the biblical doctrine of justification, particularly, that justification consists in the imputation of Christ's righteousness to the believer by grace through faith apart from any human works. In this section we set forth the position of Moral Government Theology on each of these points, documented by direct citations from leading theorists of Moral Government Theology.

1. Heresy Regarding God's Foreknowledge

a. "God does not know ahead of time the free decisions of men. . . ."[2]

---

[2] Elseth, *Did God Know?*, p. 70.

Because God's knowledge is limited to the actually knowable, God cannot know the ". . . future choices of moral beings, when acting freely in their moral agency," since these choices "have not been brought into existence as yet and thus are not fixities or objects of possible knowledge."[3]

b. "Many Bible passages, when taken in their natural meaning, appear to indicate that God does not have absolute foreknowledge over all his own future actions, nor over all those of His moral creatures."[4]

c. "Thus, God may have predictions and theories as to what man will do, but He cannot know with certainty what man will do in areas where God has given man absolute freedom of choice."[5]

d. "A significant percentage of prophecy indicating what God said He would do never took place."[6]

e. "In fact, God often changes His mind and does not do the things He says He will do."[7]

f. "The ultimate end of this tragedy is that Christians begin to believe that God is satisfactorily working out His plan as He wants it in the world."[8]

Since preparing the first edition of this document, citations from Winkie Pratney (a leading proponent of certain aspects of Moral Government Theology) on God's foreknowledge have come to our attention:

- "We even see a God Who is willing to CHANGE HIS PLANS. . . ."[9]
- "He has *deliberately chosen* to limit Himself to our free

[3] Olson, *Truth*, p. T-III-13.
[4] *Ibid.*, p. T-III-18.
[5] Elseth, *Did God Know?*, p. 97.
[6] *Ibid.*, p. 107.
[7] *Ibid.*, p. 109.
[8] *Ibid.*, p. 98.
[9] Pratney, *Youth Aflame*, 1970 ed., p. JD-17, emphases original.

response in the carrying out of His will. . . . Many of the Father's *future* decisions depend on our own."[10]

• "*God is not hindered by time* . . . [or] *resources* . . . [or] lack of *power* or *wisdom* or *ability*. He is limited *only* by those He created free who do not serve Him with a perfect heart and a willing mind . . . [sic] He is limited by MAN'S DISOBEDIENCE (Psalm 78:41). He wants YOU to help Him carry out His goal (John 20:21)."[11]

2. Heresy Regarding God's Moral Character

a. "If we say that God is simply a 'blob' of good in the sky who can do nothing but good, because He is good, you then destroy the factor of choice. . . . He only is able to do right who is able at the same time to do wrong."[12]

b. "God is good because He chooses to be good."[13]

c. ". . . the power to [choose] contrary is essential to free moral agency" and God is a free moral agent, for "The Godhead . . . possess moral freedom, or the power of self-determination or free will."[14]

d. "God is not holy because He is holy—He is holy because He chooses to use all His attributes in a loving (*agape*) way."[15]

Again, additional evidence about Winkie Pratney's views has appeared. On God's moral character, Pratney's position

---

[10] *Ibid.*, pp. JD-17-18, emphases original.

[11] *Ibid.*, p. JD-18, emphases original.

[12] Elseth, *Did God Know?*, pp. 26-7.

[13] *Ibid.*, p. 30.

[14] Olson, *Sharing*, page opposite p. W-Me-IV-6, and p. W-Me-I-2. Compare: "Moral attributes involve . . . choice. . . . They are not natural attributes in that they are not endowments of God's existence, but are moral in the sense that they are the result of a disposition of will. They exist because each Member of the Godhead perpetually chooses that they should be so" (p. W-Me-I-15), and "moral attributes of God . . . are in reality attributes of God's voluntary moral character . . ." (p. W-Me-I-19).

[15] Otis, *The God They Never Knew*, p. 38.

is less clear than Olson, Elseth, and Otis's. In conversation Pratney affirmed that he believed it was impossible for God to choose to sin. This is confirmed in one of his recent books: "[God] is, of course, faithful and changeless. We need never worry that God will one day have an ultimate character change, or that He might become bad. The Bible is clear that He is not only good, but absolutely and unchangeably loving, just and good."[16]

However, this apparently clear assertion of moral immutability in God is qualified by other statements Pratney makes in the same book. Pratney distinguishes God's moral character from His being, holding that the former is determined actively by God's choices, but that the latter is essential and completely independent of God's choices. The law that distinguishes right from wrong, Pratney, says, is "*distinct* from God's character, as *eternal* as He is and yet not separate from Him!"[17] This is because this law is an element of God's being, and it obligates God's will, which in turn defines God's character. Thus, "*God himself has a law to keep*; God himself has a standard to which He conforms His life."[18] At this point, however, Pratney's view takes on complexities that border on inconsistency and the logical implication that God is, after all, capable of choosing contrary to that law:

> As we shall see in later discussion, we were made to choose the valuable. God made us like that, because *He* is like that, and we are made in His image. He has always done what we must always do; respond to that which is the most lovely, the most important, the most worthwhile; this is the law of love. God himself unselfishly chooses the highest good of His own being; not just because it is His, but because it is the most valuable. He must. He is obligated to do so. To choose anything less would not only be unwise but wrong. And so must we. We must do what He

[16] Pratney, *The Nature and Character of God*, p. 59.
[17] *Ibid.*, p. 60.
[18] *Ibid.*, p. 59.

> has always done; put Him first, honor with our lives the revealed ultimate loveliness in the universe, and give Him the glory for what He is.[19]

Although Pratney's repeated use of the word *must* makes it appear that this means God is incapable of doing other than what is right, closer analysis gives reason to question whether that is really what Pratney means. He says that we "must" just as God "must." But are we incapable of choosing otherwise? Certainly not. Is Pratney using *must* in a moral sense in reference to man but in a metaphysical sense in reference to God? In other words, when he says that man "must . . . put Him first, honor with our lives the revealed ultimate loveliness in the universe, and give Him the glory for what He is," is he merely saying that we are morally obligated to do so but that we are capable of violating that obligation? If so, how are we to know, in the context, that he doesn't mean the same thing when he says that God "must" choose "the highest good of His own being"?

Ultimately, then, Pratney's views on the moral nature of God are at best inconsistent, as is clear from the following:

> [God] has eternally and unvaryingly chosen what He sees and knows, in infinite wisdom, to be the most valuable object in the universe: the incomparable value of His own created [*sic*; presumably Pratney here intended "uncreated"] being, the foundation of all reality. . . . When the Bible calls Him "good," it means something. God is good because He has always done what is best and unalterably always will. His law is founded in His being, not His will; it is, therefore, not arbitrary or changeable. His being is distinct from His will and its infinite value perpetually obligates His will; therefore God himself has a law to keep. Love is not just something He invented. It is the way of supreme intelligence, the way God chooses to live and the way He asks all to live likewise.[20]

---

[19] *Ibid.*, p. 60, emphasis original.
[20] *Ibid.*, p. 61.

In *Youth Aflame*, an earlier book, Pratney strongly implied that God's moral character was subject to choice and that God was capable of choosing wrongly: ". . . God made us in the finite, miniature likeness of Himself—able to *choose*, free to do right or wrong."[21] In personal conversation, Pratney claimed that by placing the dash in the sentence he intended to indicate that the description that followed it of *our* ability to choose between right and wrong did not apply to God. That explanation, however consistent it might be with what Pratney thinks today, hardly seems credible as an explanation of his intent when he first wrote the sentence, in light of other things Pratney wrote of God then:

> We have already seen that God has an infinitely great Being and is an indescribably lovely Person. Now the next amazing thing we find out about God is that He is like this because He has *chosen* to be! God *Himself* has a law to keep.
>
> God didn't just "make up" this law. It has *always* been in the Universe as long as God *Himself* has been here, because it is something just naturally true about His life....
>
> You know that God *thinks* . . . and *feels* like us. . . . He can also *CHOOSE* between two things. . . . He can *originate* choice. These qualities make up what we call His *MORAL* ATTRIBUTES. He *can* control what He does. He has power over His *own* power, to make amazing and infinitely wise decisions, directed by these powers of His incredibly wonderful personality.
>
> But God's *BEING* functions quite apart from His *character*. He did not *create* this; He has *always* had this spiritual, self-existent Being, just like *we* have a body to live in. This infinite Being is distinct from His personality. Out of its powers He fashioned man and his world. . . . Since everyone's happiness *depends* on these powers, God *Himself* has a responsibility to take care for them. And here is the *ultimate basis* of God's law. Since everyone's life hangs on *His* well-being, God MUST *will His own highest good* as

[21] Pratney, *Youth Aflame*, 1970 ed., p. JD-17, emphasis original.

> the *wisest possible* act. If He decided otherwise, He would be unwise; His infinitely wonderful mind has never made a foolish choice. He is *obliged* to rule Himself and His creation for *everyone's* highest good. Just as *we* are responsible to love and take care of our lives, God is responsible to love and take care of *His*.[22]

And:

> God is good because He always *keeps* this law of valueableness [*sic*]. That is why *we* should all choose it, just as God does. God's love-law is *founded in His Being, not His will*. Since His being is *separate* from His will, the law *obligates* His will; He himself can *choose* to be good. That is why the words "God is love" mean something when applied to God. God has a law to keep Himself, and He keeps it. "Love" is not just something He invented. It is the way of a supremely intelligent life, and it is the way God *chose* to live.[23]

3. Heresy Regarding Sin

a. "All sin consists in sinning—there can be no moral character but in moral acts."[24]

b. "We search in vain for any evidence that would indicate that sin is a substance or anything other than a wrong moral choice."[25]

c. "IF it [the mind] should not know the choice is bad, it is NOT SIN to the individual!"[26] "There is therefore, no such thing as 'unconscious' sin. God holds us responsible for all the light we have and are able to get—no more, no less. There is no sin that we know nothing at all about that God will judge us for."[27]

---

[22] *Ibid.*, p. JS-8, emphases original.
[23] *Ibid.*, pp. JD-8-9, emphases original.
[24] Olson, *Sharing*, unnumbered page opposite p. W-Me-IV-6.
[25] Otis, *The God They Never Knew*, p. 63.
[26] Pratney, *Youth Aflame!*, 1983, p. 83, emphases original.
[27] *Ibid.*, p. 93.

d. "Moral depravity . . . is always a voluntary development. . . . The universality of sin in the world is not to be accounted for, therefore, by some fixed causation in our personality inherited by birth. . . ."[28]

e. ". . . a contradiction would exist in the Bible if any statement could be found declaring our guilt for Adam's sin."[29] "If the Bible affirmed that we are held accountable for other's (*sic*) sins, and particularly for Adam's sin, this would become such a gross injustice in the economy of God as to erect a barrier to intelligent thought and the meaning of guilt."[30]

f. "This [moral depravity] is what we *do* with our situation, unintelligent responses to influences and suggestions. *This is sin*, but it is *not inherited*—it comes by *choice*, it is *created*."[31] "We are all victims of physical depravity and death, circumstances and environments that provide powerful temptations to sin, and *all men* follow the wrong choice of our first parents. Our own family lines, and ultimately Adam himself are responsible for our PHYSICAL depravity. But this is, in itself, *not* sin. It is not the direct CAUSE of sin, so that we sin from some sort of physical *necessity*, but simply the weakened constitution and strong desires that give sin power and make men open to the tug of temptation."[32]

g. "We cannot say we were unable to fulfill God's reasonable and loving requirements."[33] "*Physical depravity* gives great power to temptation. We cannot *help* our physical nature, and God does not *condemn* us for being born in such a condition without choice."[34]

h. "Evidently, man is able to rise up to do battle with himself in turning away from sin, for God commands 'all

---

[28] Olson, *Sharing*, pp. W-Me-IV-4-5.
[29] *Ibid.*, p. W-Me-IV-5.
[30] *Ibid.*, p. W-Me-VII-3.
[31] Otis, *The God They Never Knew*, p. 59, emphases added.
[32] Pratney, *Youth Aflame!*, p. 76, emphases original.
[33] Olson, *Sharing*, p. W-Me-VII-3.
[34] Pratney, *Youth Aflame!*, p. 94, emphases original.

men everywhere to repent' (Acts 17:30) and nowhere implies that he is unable to do so."[35]

i. "So-called inability is a question of 'will not' rather than 'cannot' obey God's reasonable requirements."[36]

j. "Falling short of the mark doesn't prove it out of range; the aim may not have been high enough."[37]

Yet again, we have found additional evidence of Pratney's views since preparing the first edition of this document:

> Many think they have *explained* the fact of sin in the human race by using a phrase we shall call "Doggie Logic." It goes essentially like this: "A *dog* is not a dog *because* he barks; he barks *because* he *is* a dog. Thus, man is not a sinner because he *sins*; he sins *because* he *is* a sinner." The assumption is, of course, that all sin flows from a *pre-determined sinful nature*, and it is *this* nature that creates sinful acts of the sinner. Just as the bark of a dog comes undeniably from the fact that he *is* a dog, so man's sin will flow inescapably from the fact that he *is* a sinner, and was *born* so. It *sounds* nice; is it *true*?
>
> There are, unfortunately, *two things wrong* with this logic. They are *serious* flaws, because once they are *assumed*, they actually *destroy* the basis of the very thing they seek to prove—that all men are *guilty* of, and *responsible* to God for, their sin. These logic flaws are—[a] *A Man is not a dog.* A dog's actions are *right* if he barks, because God *created* dogs to express themselves naturally by barking. But God did *not* create men to *sin*! A dog's bark is *natural*; sin is *NOT*. . . . Assuming that man sins *because* it is his *nature* to sin, also assumes that *sin* is natural. . . . If a man sins, it merely proves that he has so chosen to sin, and his sin will certainly be treated as *unnatural* in the eyes of God. [b] *Do we need a sinful nature to sin*? Is it *necessary* to have an "implanted sinfulness" to enable man to do wrong? If *one* sin-

[35] Olson, *Sharing*, p. W-Me-IV-4.

[36] *Ibid.*, p. W-Me-VIII-6.

[37] Pratney, *Youth Aflame!*, p. 93.

ner can be found in Scripture who sinned WITHOUT first having a sinful nature, the answer is *no*, and the case is closed. And of course, there are at least *three* moral beings who committed sin without sinful natures [Satan, Adam, and Eve].[38]

Again:

> *Sin is ORIGINAL*—There is nothing clearer in the Bible that man is VERY original in his sin! Sin is not a *transmitted* thing; it is *created* by each being with the elements of true morality—(emotions; reason, free will, moral light and spiritual perception of this).[39]

Again:

> From this study of Bible words describing sin, we look *in vain* for evidence that sin is anything else than a *wrong choice*. There is always the idea of *movement*, *voluntary action*, *never* a static or inactive something *behind* the will, received by heredity, that CAUSES the will to act in sin. The Word of God protects itself from theological speculation like this; sin is a CHOICE.
>
> *Without God*, man *does* have a sinful nature, but this nature is *NOT* physical. He inherits no causation from his parents or anyone else. Man is responsible for his *own* actions. His sinful nature consists in the *habit patterns* of a life lived for *self* instead of *God*.[40]

And again:

> It may be objected—does not the *Bible* teach that man is *born* sinful? The answer is an unqualified *no*.[41]

---

[38] Pratney, *Youth Aflame*, 1970 ed., p. JS-13, emphases original.
[39] *Ibid.*, p. JS-16, emphases original.
[40] *Ibid.*, p. JS-17, emphases original.
[41] *Ibid.*, p. JS-19, emphases original.

4. Heresy Regarding the Atonement

a. "Contrary to warped speculation, God was never worried about receiving some personal satisfaction for the hurt sin has caused Him."[42]

b. "The sacrifice of Christ is not the payment of a debt, nor is it a complete satisfaction of justice for sin."[43]

c. "God is willing to forgive man's sin 'freely by His grace,' without any need for personal vindictive satisfaction."[44] "There is a willingness to forgive rather than an insistence upon vindictive satisfaction . . . a bypassing of personal justice rather than a demanding of punishment."[45]

d. "One of the deceiver's most damaging deceptions centers around—of all events—the atonement. . . . The idea perpetrated here probably is derived from the words 'ransom' and 'redeem' and it is that Jesus *paid* for our sins."[46] "The assertion that Jesus *paid* for our sins has caused immeasurable damage to the body of Christ."[47] "If we accept the premise that Jesus literally purchased our salvation with His blood, it . . . portrays God as vindictive and bloodthirsty. . . ."[48]

e. "God does not require an exact payment for sin to satisfy retributive justice. . . . 'God is love' and has completely subdued all thought of retaliation toward rebellious sinners."[49]

5. Heresy Regarding Justification

a. "The active obedience or holiness of Christ . . . is not legally imputed to the believer."[50] "The theological doctrine of 'imputed righteousness' has been grossly distorted in our day. We are told that God looks at us through the blood of

---

[42] Otis, *The God They Never Knew*, p. 97.
[43] Olson, *Sharing*, p. 2.
[44] *Ibid.*, p. W-Me-VI-1.
[45] *Ibid.*, p. W-Me-VI-1.
[46] Otis, *The God They Never Knew*, p. 26, emphasis original.
[47] *Ibid.*, p. 93, emphasis original.
[48] *Ibid.*, p. 109.
[49] Olson, *Sharing*, p. W-Me-V-4.
[50] *Ibid.*, p. 2.

Christ—and sees us as righteous, regardless of our actual state. Let's stop kidding ourselves. God sees us exactly the way we are."[51]

b. "The notion that God enjoys fellowship with those who are sinners by glancing at Christ's righteousness beside Him is abstract, inconceivable, unrealistic and requires long writings to explain!"[52]

c. "Repentance is the condition of, or the *prerequisite to*, salvation."[53] "Repentance doesn't mean that we cease to be guilty, but that we cease to sin."[54] "The eternal happiness of heaven can only become a reality, therefore, by the elimination of all sin. Where is sin eliminated? . . . in this life of probation."[55]

d. "Our trite little formula 'just accept Jesus' has produced countless spiritual stillbirths and inoculated millions of others against the true gospel. . . . It is not the matter of whether or not we 'accept Christ' but whether or not Christ accepts us—that is the crucial issue. Will, indeed, Christ accept us the way we are as so many today infer? Will the King of kings come in to rule over a garbage dump? The notion that the sinner's condition is irrelevant at salvation only reveals our ignorance of God and the nature of the salvation process."[56]

e. "Antinomianism [is] the concept that faith alone, without obedience to moral law, is all that is necessary for salvation (Considered by sound theologians to be erroneous doctrine based on a misconception of what salvation really is)."[57]

f "Because of a free will I myself am ultimately responsible for my salvation."[58]

---

[51] Otis, *The God They Never Knew*, p. 43.

[52] *Ibid.*, p. 142.

[53] *Ibid.*, p. 136, emphasis original.

[54] *Ibid.*, p. 155.

[55] Olson, *Sharing*, p. W-Me-VIII-3.

[56] Otis, *The God They Never Knew*, p. 141.

[57] Conn, ed., *Finney's Systematic Theology*, p. 427.

[58] Elseth, *Did God Know?*, p. 108.

Section II: The Biblical System Set Forth

Scripture contradicts each and every essential point of Moral Government Theology. It affirms (1) God's absolute and unchangeable foreknowledge, including His perfect foreknowledge of all acts of men and all His own acts; (2) God's absolute and unchangeable goodness; (3) the doctrines of original sin and human moral inability; (4) that the atonement consists in Christ's paying sinners' debt and bearing their punishment for sin as their substitute in satisfaction of the demands of God's justice; and (5) that believers are justified by grace alone through faith alone in the atoning work of Christ and have the righteousness of Christ imputed to them.

In each of the subpoints to the following five sections, we will see the direct contradiction between Scripture and the teachings of Moral Government Theology presented in the same subpoints to the five sections above.

1. The Biblical Doctrine of God's Foreknowledge

a. "For Jesus knew from the beginning who they were who did not believe, and who it was that would betray Him" (John 6:64). "I know the ones I have chosen; but it is that the Scripture may be fulfilled, 'He who eats My bread has lifted up his heel against Me.' From now on I am telling you before it comes to pass, so that when it does occur, you may believe that I am [He]" (John 13:18-19).[59] "Truly, truly I say to you, a cock shall not crow, until you deny Me three times" (John 13:38). "Then David said, 'Will the men of Keilah surrender me and my men into the hand of Saul?' And the LORD said, 'They will surrender you'" (1 Sam. 23:12).

---

[59] Note that *He* at the close of the verse is not in the Greek text. The final Greek clause, *ego eimi*, asserts Christ's eternal existence. Compare Exodus 3:14; Isaiah 43:10. Thus Christ presents His absolute foreknowledge of the one who would betray Him as evidence of His deity. It would not be such evidence if His foreknowledge did not differ qualitatively from man's predictive abilities. Not a mere probability, but a certainty of prediction is in mind here.

b. "Great is our Lord, . . . His understanding is infinite" (Ps. 147:5). "God . . . calls the things which do not exist as existing" (Rom. 4:17).[60] "I am the first and I am the last, and there is no God besides Me. And who is like Me? Let him proclaim and declare it; yes, let him recount it to Me in order, from the time that I established the ancient nation. And let them declare to them the things that are coming and the events that are going to take place. Do not tremble and do not be afraid; have I not long since announced it to you and declared it?" (Is. 44:6-8) "Thus says the LORD, the Holy One of Israel, and his Maker: 'Ask Me about the things to come concerning My sons, and you shall commit to Me the work of My hands. It is I who made the earth, and created man upon it. I stretched out the heavens with My hands, and I ordained all their host. I have aroused [Cyrus][61] in righteousness, and I will make all his ways smooth; he will build My city, and will let My exiles go free, without any payment or reward,' says the LORD of hosts" (Is. 45:11-13). "I am God, and there is no one like Me, declaring the end from the beginning and from ancient times things which have not been done" (Is. 46:9-10).

c. "I am God, and there is no one like Me, declaring the end from the beginning and from ancient times things which have not been done, saying, 'My purpose will be established, and I will accomplish all My good pleasure'; calling a bird of prey from the east, the man of My purpose from a far country. Truly I have spoken; truly I will bring it to pass. I have planned it, surely I will do it" (Is. 46:9-11). "[God] works all things after the counsel of His will" (Eph. 1:11).

d. "When a prophet speaks in the name of the LORD, if the thing does not come about or come true, that is the thing

---

[60] *NASB* margin; compare *NIV* text: "God . . . calls things that are not as though they were;" *AV* text: "God . . . calleth those things which are not as though they were."

[61] See Isaiah 45:1.

which the LORD has not spoken. The prophet has spoken it presumptuously; you shall not be afraid of him" (Deut. 18:22). "I am God, and there is no one like Me, declaring the end from the beginning and from ancient times things which have not been done, saying, 'My purpose will be established, and I will accomplish all My good pleasure'; calling a bird of prey from the east, the man of My purpose from a far country. Truly I have spoken; truly I will bring it to pass. I have planned it, surely I will do it" (Is. 46:9-11). "[God] works all things after the counsel of His will" (Eph. 1:11).

e. "God is not a man, that He should lie, nor a son of man, that He should repent; has He said, and will He not do it? Or has He spoken, and will He not make it good?" (Num. 23:19). "And also the glory of Israel will not lie or change His mind; for He is not a man that He should change His mind" (1 Sam. 15:29). "Truly I have spoken; truly I will bring it to pass. I have planned it, surely I will do it" (Is. 46:9-11).

f. "[God] works all things after the counsel of His will" (Eph. 1:11). "I am God, and there is no one like Me, declaring the end from the beginning and from ancient times things which have not been done, saying, 'My purpose will be established, and I will accomplish all My good pleasure'; calling a bird of prey from the east, the man of My purpose from a far country. Truly I have spoken; truly I will bring it to pass. I have planned it, surely I will do it" (Is. 46:9-11). "And we know that God causes all things to work together for good to those who love God, to those who are called according to His purpose" (Rom. 8:28). "I know that Thou canst do all things, and that no purpose of Thine can be thwarted" (Job 42:2).

2. The Biblical Doctrine of God's Moral Character

a. "God is love" (1 John 4:16).[62] "[God] cannot deny Himself" (2 Tim. 2:13). "God, who cannot lie" (Tit. 1:2). "God is

---

[62] The anarthrous predicate nominative *agape*, preceding the verb, emphasizes the *nature* of the subject: God is loving *by nature.* On the qualita-

light, and in Him there is no darkness at all" (1 John 1:5).[63] "God, desiring even more to show to the heirs of the promise the unchangeableness of His purpose, interposed with an oath, in order that by two unchangeable things in which it is impossible for God to lie, we may have strong encouragement, we who have fled for refuge in laying hold of the hope set before us" (Heb. 6:17-18).

b. "Thou art good and doest good" (Ps. 119:68).[64]

c. "Thine eyes are too pure to approve evil, and Thou canst not look on wickedness with favor" (Hab. 1:13).

d. "Let no one say when he is tempted, 'I am being tempted by God'; for God cannot be tempted by evil, and He Himself does not tempt anyone" (Jas. 1:13). "For I, the LORD, do not change; therefore you, O sons of Jacob, are not consumed" (Mal. 3:6).

3. The Biblical Doctrine of Sin

a. "For while we were in the flesh, the sinful passions, which were aroused by the Law, were at work in the members of our body to bear fruit for death. . . . But sin, taking opportunity through the commandment, produced in me coveting of every kind; for apart from the Law sin is dead. And I was once alive apart from the Law; but when the commandment came, sin became alive, and I died; . . . for sin, taking opportunity through the commandment, deceived me, and through it killed me. . . . it was sin [that became a cause of death for me], in order that it might be shown to be sin by effecting my death through that which is good, that through the commandment sin might become utterly sinful. For we know that the Law is spiritual; but I am of flesh, sold

---

tive emphasis of the anarthrous predicate nominative, see Philip B. Harner, "Qualitative Anarthrous Predicate Nouns; Mark 15:39 and John 1:1," *Journal of Biblical Literature* 92 (March 1973), pp. 75-87.

[63] The anarthrous predicate nominative *phos*, preceding the verb, emphasizes the *nature* of the subject: God is light *by nature*. See previous note.

[64] See page 30 (chap. 1, footnote 29).

into bondage to sin. . . . So now, no longer am I the one doing [the very thing I do not wish to do], but sin which indwells me. . . . But if I am doing the very thing I do not wish, I am no longer the one doing it, but sin which dwells in me. I find then the principle that evil is present in me, the one who wishes to do good. For I joyfully concur with the law of God in the inner man, but I see a different law in the members of my body, waging war against the law of my mind, and making me a prisoner of the law of sin which is in my members" (Rom. 7:5-23). "The heart is more deceitful than all else and is desperately sick; who can understand it?" (Jer. 17:9) "then the LORD saw that the wickedness of man was great on the earth, and that every intent of the thoughts of his heart was only evil continually" (Gen. 6:5). ". . . the intent of man's heart is evil from his youth" (Gen. 8:21).[65]

b. "If we say that we have no sin, we are deceiving ourselves. . . . If we say that we have not sinned, we make Him a liar" (1 John 1:8a, 10a).[66]

c. "If a person sins unintentionally in any of the things which the LORD has commanded not to be done, and commits any of them, . . . then let him offer to the LORD a bull without defect as a sin offering for the sin he has committed" (Lev. 4:2-3). "When a leader sins and unintentionally does any of all the things which the LORD God has commanded not to be done, and he becomes guilty, if his sin which he has committed is made known to him, he shall bring for his offering a goat, . . . it is a sin offering" (Lev. 4:22-24). "Now if anyone of the common people sins unintentionally . . . and becomes guilty, if his sin . . . is made known to him, then he

---

[65] "By heart in scriptural language is meant the man himself; the soul; that which is the seat and source of life. . . . It never signifies a mere act, or a transient state of the soul. It is that which is abiding, which determines character." Hodge, *Systematic Theology*, 2:240.

[66] Note the difference between having sin (the principle) and having sinned (the act). Both are real. If we deny the reality of the sin principle "we are deceiving ourselves."

shall bring for his offering a goat . . ." (Leviticus 4:27-28). "If a person acts unfaithfully and sins unintentionally against the LORD's holy things, then he shall bring his guilt offering to the LORD . . ." (Lev. 5:15). "I am conscious of nothing against myself, yet I am not by this acquitted; but the one who examines me is the Lord" (1 Cor. 4:4).

d. "And you, being dead in your trespasses and sins, . . . were *by nature* children of wrath" (Eph. 2:1 [*NASB* margin], 3, emphasis added). "For as through the one man's disobedience, the many were *made sinners* . . ." (Rom. 5:19, emphasis added). "For as in Adam all die . . ." (1 Cor. 15:22). "Among [the sons of disobedience] we too *all* formerly lived . . ." (Eph. 2:3, *cf.* 2:2, emphasis added).[67] "Grapes are not gathered from thorn bushes, nor figs from thistles, are they? Even so, every good tree bears good fruit; but the bad tree bears bad fruit. A good tree cannot produce bad fruit, nor can a bad tree produce good fruit" (Matt. 7:16-18). ". . . all have sinned and fall short of the glory of God" (Rom. 3:23).

e. ". . . the judgment arose from one transgression resulting in condemnation. . . . by the transgression of the one, death reigned through the one. . . . through one transgression there resulted condemnation to all men . . ." (Rom. 5:16-18).

f. "And you were dead in your trespasses and sins, in which you formerly walked according to the course of this world, according to the prince of the power of the air, of the spirit that is now working in the sons of disobedience. Among them we too all formerly lived in the lusts of our flesh indulging the desires of the flesh and of the mind, and were *by nature* children of wrath, even as the rest" (Eph. 2:1-3, emphasis added). "The wicked are estranged from the womb; these who

---

[67] The "moral genitive" (Lenski's term) *sons of disobedience* expresses the very nature of the persons in mind. They are disobedient by nature. It is their very nature to disobey; it is not a characteristic that they develop by means of disobeying. See R. C. H. Lenski, *The Interpretation of St. Paul's Epistles to the Galatians, Ephesians and Philippians* (Minneapolis, MN: Augsburg, [1946] 1961), pp. 407-13.

speak lies go astray from birth" (Ps. 58:3). "Behold, I was brought forth in iniquity, and in sin my mother conceived me" (Ps. 51:5). "What is man, that he should be pure, or he who is born of a woman, that he should be righteous?" (Job 15:14) "How then can a man be just with God? Or how can he be clean who is born of woman?" (Job 25:4).

g. "And you were *dead in your trespasses and sins*, in which you formerly walked according to the course of this world, according to the prince of the power of the air, of the spirit that is now working in the sons of disobedience. Among them we too all formerly lived in the lusts of our flesh, indulging the desires of the flesh and of the mind, and were *by nature children of wrath*, even as the rest" (Eph. 2:1-3, emphasis added). "A good tree cannot produce bad fruit, nor can a bad tree produce good fruit" (Matt. 7:18). "But thanks be to God that though you *were slaves of sin*, you became obedient from the heart to that form of teaching to which you were committed, and *having been freed from sin*, you became slaves of righteousness" (Rom. 6:17-18, emphasis added). "For when you were slaves of sin, you were free in regard to righteousness" (Rom. 6:20). "For the law of the Spirit of life in Christ Jesus has *set you free from the law of sin and of death*. For what the Law *could not do, weak as it was through the flesh*, God did: sending His own Son in the likeness of sinful flesh and as an offering for sin, He condemned sin in the flesh, in order that the requirement of the Law might be fulfilled in us, who do not walk according to the flesh, but according to the Spirit. *For those who are according to the flesh set their minds on the things of the flesh*, but those who are according to the Spirit, the things of the Spirit. For the mind set on the flesh is death, but the mind set on the Spirit is life and peace, because the mind set on the flesh is hostile toward God; for it does not subject itself to the law of God, for it is *not even able to do so*; and those who are in the flesh *cannot please God*" (Rom. 8:2-8, emphases added). "That which is born of the flesh is flesh, and that which is born of the Spirit is spirit" (John 3:6).

h. "And you were *dead* in your trespasses and sins, . . . sons of disobedience . . . by nature children of wrath, even as the rest. But God, being rich in mercy, because of His great love with which He loved us, even when we were *dead* in our transgressions, *made us alive together with Christ* (by grace you have been saved), and raised us up with Him, and seated us with Him in the heavenly places, in Christ Jesus, in order that in the ages to come He might show the surpassing riches of His grace in kindness toward us in Christ Jesus. For by grace you have been saved through faith; and that not of yourselves, it is the gift of God; not as a result of works, that no one should boast. For we are His workmanship, created in Christ Jesus for good works, which God prepared beforehand, that we should walk in them" (Eph. 2:1-10, emphases added). "I am of flesh, sold into bondage to sin" (Rom. 7:14). "For I know that nothing good dwells in me, that is, in my flesh; for the wishing is present in me, but the doing of the good is not. For the good that I wish, I do not do; but I practice the very evil that I do not wish. But if I am doing the very thing I do not wish, I am no longer the one doing it, but sin which dwells in me. I find then the principle that evil is present in me, the one who wishes to do good. For I joyfully concur with the law of God in the inner man, but I see a different law in the members of my body, waging war against the law of my mind, and making me a prisoner of the law of sin which is in my members. Wretched man that I am! Who will set me free from the body of this death? Thanks be to God through Jesus Christ our Lord!" (Rom. 7:18-25)

i. "A good tree cannot produce bad fruit, nor can a bad tree produce good fruit" (Matt. 7:18). "But thanks be to God that though you *were slaves of sin*, you became obedient from the heart to that form of teaching to which you were committed, and *having been freed from sin*, you became slaves of righteousness" (Rom. 6:17-18). "For when you were slaves of sin, you were free in regard to righteousness" (Rom. 6:20). "For the law of the Spirit of life in Christ Jesus has *set you free from the law of sin and of death*. For what the Law *could not do, weak as it was through the flesh*, God did: sending His own Son in the likeness of sinful flesh and as an offering for sin, He condemned sin in the flesh, in order that the requirement of the Law might be fulfilled in us, who do not walk according to the flesh, but according to the Spirit. *For those who are according to the flesh set their minds on the things of the flesh*, but those who are according to the Spirit, the things of the Spirit. For the mind set on the flesh is death, but the mind set on the Spirit is life and peace, because the mind set on the flesh is hostile toward God; for it does not subject itself to the law of God, for it is *not even able to do so*; and those who are in the flesh *cannot please God*" (Rom. 8:2-8, emphases added). "That which is born of the flesh is flesh, and that which is born of the Spirit is spirit" (John 3:6).

j. "For the mind set on the flesh is death, but the mind set on the Spirit is life and peace, because the mind set on the flesh is hostile toward God; for it does not subject itself to the law of God, for it is *not even able to do so*; and those who are in the flesh *cannot please God*" (Rom. 8:2-8, emphases added). "That which is born of the flesh is flesh, and that which is born of the Spirit is spirit" (John 3:6).

4. The Biblical Doctrine of the Atonement

a. "I, the LORD your God, am a jealous God, visiting the iniquity of the fathers on the children, on the third and the fourth generations of those who hate Me . . . the LORD will not leave him unpunished who takes His name in vain" (Ex. 20:5, 7). "[If anyone says,] 'I have peace though I walk in the stubbornness of my heart . . .,' [t]he LORD shall never be willing to forgive him, but rather the anger of the LORD and His jealousy will burn against that man, and every curse which is written in this book will rest on him, and the LORD will blot out his name from under heaven" (Deut. 29:19-20). "You will not be able to serve the LORD, for He is a holy God. He is a jealous God; He will not forgive your transgression or your sins. If you forsake the LORD and serve foreign gods, then He will turn and do you harm and consume you after He has done good to you" (Josh. 24:19-20). "A jealous and avenging God is the LORD; the LORD is avenging and wrathful. The LORD takes vengeance on His adversaries, and He reserves wrath for His enemies. The LORD is slow to anger and great in power, and the LORD will by no means leave the guilty unpunished" (Nah. 1:2-3). "Vengeance is Mine, and retribution . . ." (Deut. 32:35). "'Vengeance is Mine, I will repay,' says the Lord" (Rom. 12:19). "For God will bring every act to judgment, everything which is hidden, whether it is good or evil" (Eccl. 12:14). "And we know that the judgment of God rightly falls upon those who practice [evil] things. And do you suppose . . . that you will escape the judgment of God? . . . But because of your stubbornness and unrepentant heart you are storing up wrath for yourself in the day of wrath and revelation of the righteous judgment of God, who will render to every man according to his deeds: to those who by perseverance in doing good seek for glory and honor and immortality, eternal life; but to those who are selfishly ambitious and do not obey the truth, but obey unrighteousness, wrath and indignation. . . . For there is no partiality with God" (Rom. 2:2-3, 5-8). "The God who inflicts wrath is not unrighteous, is He? (I am speaking in human terms.) May it never be! For otherwise how will God judge the world?" (Rom. 3:5-6) "[F]or all have sinned and fall short of the glory of God, being justified as a gift by His grace through the redemption which is in Christ Jesus; whom God displayed publicly as a *propitiation*[68] in His blood through faith. This was to demonstrate His righteousness, because in the forbearance of God He passed over the sins previously committed; for the demonstration, I say, of His righteousness at the present time, that He might be just and the justifier of the one who has faith in Jesus" (Rom. 3:23-26). "For the wages of sin is

[68] See chap. 1, footnote 31.

death" (Rom. 6:23). "[A]nd He Himself is the propitiation[69] for our sins" (1 John 2:2).

b. "And when you were dead in your transgressions and the uncircumcision of your flesh, He made you alive together with Him, having forgiven us all our transgressions, having canceled out the certificate of debt consisting of decrees against us and which was hostile to us; and He has taken it out of the way, having nailed it to the cross" (Col. 2:13-14).

c. "[F]or all have sinned and fall short of the glory of God, being justified as a gift by His grace through the redemption which is in Christ Jesus; whom God displayed publicly as a *propitiation*[70] in His blood through faith. This was to demonstrate His righteousness, because in the forbearance of God He passed over the sins previously committed; for the demonstration, I say, of His righteousness at the present time, that He might be just and the justifier of the one who has faith in Jesus" (Rom. 3:23-26).

d. "[Y]ou were not redeemed[71] with perishable things . . . but with precious[72] blood, as of a lamb unblemished and spotless, the blood of Christ" (1 Pet. 1:18-19). "[T]he Son of Man did not come to be served, but to serve, and to give His life a ransom[73] for many" (Matt. 20:28). "In Him we have redemption[74] through His blood, the forgiveness of our trespasses, according to the riches of His grace" (Eph. 1:7). "[The Holy Spirit] is given as a pledge[75] of our inheritance, with a view to the redemption[76] of God's own possession" (Eph. 1:14). "[Christ] gave Himself for us, that He might redeem[77] us from

[69] Greek hilasmos, "propitiation, expiation," Bauer, *A Greek-English Lexicon*, p. 375. See chap. 1, footnote 31.

[70] See footnote 69 above.

[71] See chap. 1, footnote 32.

[72] See chap. 1, footnote 33.

[73] See chap. 1, footnote 34.

[74] See chap. 1, footnote 35.

[75] See chap. 1, footnote 36.

[76] See chap. 1, footnote 37.

[77] See chap. 1, footnote 38.

every lawless deed" (Tit. 2:14). "Worthy art Thou to take the book, and to break its seals; for Thou wast slain, and didst purchase[78] for God with Thy blood men from every tribe and tongue and people and nation" (Rev. 5:9).

e. ". . . without the shedding of blood there is no forgiveness" (Heb. 9:22). ". . . the LORD will not leave him unpunished who takes His name in vain" (Ex. 20:7). "[If anyone says,] 'I have peace though I walk in the stubbornness of my heart . . .,' [t]he LORD shall never be willing to forgive him, but rather the anger of the LORD and His jealousy will burn against that man, and every curse which is written in this book will rest on him, and the LORD will blot out his name from under heaven" (Deut. 29:19-20). "A jealous and avenging God is the LORD; the LORD is avenging and wrathful. The LORD takes vengeance on His adversaries and He reserves wrath for His enemies. The LORD is slow to anger and great in power and the LORD will by no means leave the guilty unpunished" (Nah. 1:2-3). "For God will bring every act to judgment, everything which is hidden, whether it is good or evil" (Eccl. 12:14).

5. The Biblical Doctrine of Justification

a. "For if by the transgression of the one, death reigned through the one, much more those who receive the abundance of grace and of the gift of righteousness will reign in life through the One, Jesus Christ. So then as through one transgression there resulted condemnation to all men, even so through one act of righteousness there resulted justification of life to all men. For as through the one man's disobedience the many were made sinners, even so through the obedience of the One the many will be made righteous" (Rom. 5:17-19). "But to the one who does not work, but believes in Him who justifies the ungodly, his faith is reckoned[79] as

[78] See chap. 1, footnote 39.

[79] Greek *logizetai*, from *logizomai*, "reckon, calculate, count, take into account . . . evaluate, estimate, look upon as, consider," or "place to one's account," or "credit," Bauer, *A Greek-English Lexicon*, pp. 475-6.

righteousness, just as David also speaks of the blessing upon the man to whom God reckons righteousness apart from works: 'Blessed are those whose lawless deeds have been forgiven, and whose sins have been covered. Blessed is the man whose sin the Lord will not take into account'" (Rom. 4:5-7). "What shall we say then? That Gentiles, who did not pursue righteousness, attained righteousness, even the righteousness which is by faith; but Israel, pursuing a law of righteousness, did not arrive at that law. Why? Because they did not pursue it by faith, but as though it were by works. They stumbled over the stumbling stone" (Rom. 9:30-32). "But by His doing you are in Christ Jesus, who became to us wisdom from God and righteousness and sanctification, and redemption, that, just as it is written, 'Let him who boasts, boast in the Lord'" (1 Cor. 1:30-31).

b. "I count all things to be loss in view of the surpassing value of knowing Christ Jesus my Lord, for whom I have suffered the loss of all things, and count them but rubbish in order that I may gain Christ, and may be found in Him, *not having a righteousness of my own derived from the Law but that which is through faith in Christ, the righteousness which comes from God on the basis of faith*" (Phil. 3:8-9, emphasis added).

c. "For all have sinned and fall[80] short of the glory of God, being justified as a gift by His grace through the redemption which is in Christ Jesus" (Rom. 3:23-24). "And you were dead in your trespasses and sin . . . the sons of disobedience . . . by nature the children of wrath, even as the rest. But God, . . . even when we were dead in our transgressions, made us alive together with Christ . . . in order that in the ages to come He might show the surpassing riches of His grace. . . . For by grace you have been saved through faith; and that not of yourselves, it is the gift of God; not as a result of works, that no one should boast. For we are His workmanship, created in Christ Jesus for good works, which God prepared

---

[80] Greek present tense emphasizes continuing action.

beforehand, that we should walk in them" (Eph. 2:1-5, 7-10). The Greek word for *repent* is *metanoeo*, to "change one's mind, . . .then feel remorse, repent, be converted," and the word for *repentance* is *metanoia*, "a change of mind."[81] Neither means "cease to sin."

d. "But as many as received[82] Him, to them He gave the right to become children of God, even to those who believe in His name, who were born not of blood, nor of the will of the flesh, nor of the will of man, but of God" (John 1:12-13). "For while we were still helpless, at the right time Christ died for the ungodly. . . . But God demonstrates His own love toward us, in that while we were yet sinners, Christ died for us. . . . For if while we were enemies, we were reconciled to God through the death of His Son, much more, having been reconciled, we shall be saved by His life" (Rom. 5:6, 8, 10). "[E]ven when we were dead in our transgressions, [God] made us alive together with Christ" (Eph. 2:5).

e. "For we maintain that a man is justified by faith apart from works of the Law" (Rom. 3:28). "For the promise to Abraham or to his descendants that he would be heir of the world was not through the Law, but through the righteousness of faith. For if those who are of the Law are heirs, faith is made void and the promise is nullified; for the Law brings about wrath. . . . For this reason it is by faith, that it might be in accordance with grace, in order that the promise may be certain to all the descendants, not only to those who are of the Law, but also to those who are of the faith of Abraham, who is the father of us all" (Rom. 4:13-16). "Even so Abraham believed God, and it was reckoned to him as righteousness. Therefore be sure that it is those who are of faith who are sons of Abraham. And the Scripture, foreseeing that God would justify the Gentiles by faith, preached the gospel be-

---

[81] Bauer, *A Greek-English Lexicon*, pp. 511-12.

[82] Greek *elabon*, from *lambano*, "take in the hand, take hold of, grasp," "recieve, accept," "take up," "choose, select," "make one's own, apprehend or comprehend," *Ibid.*, pp. 464-5.

forehand to Abraham, saying, 'All the nations shall be blessed in you.' So then those who are of faith are blessed with Abraham, the believer. For as many as are of the works of the Law are under a curse; for it is written, 'Cursed is everyone who does not abide by all things written in the book of the law, to perform them.' Now that no one is justified by the Law before God is evident; for, 'The righteous man shall live by faith.' However, the Law is not of faith; on the contrary, 'He who practices them shall live by them.' Christ redeemed us from the curse of the Law, having become a curse for us—for it is written, 'Cursed is everyone who hangs on a tree'—in order that in Christ Jesus the blessing of Abraham might come to the Gentiles, so that we might receive the promise of the Spirit through faith. . . . For if the inheritance is based on law, it is no longer based on a promise; but God has granted it to Abraham by means of a promise. Why the Law then? It was added because of transgressions, having been ordained through angels by the agency of a mediator, until the seed should come to whom the promise had been made. . . . Is the Law then contrary to the promises of God? May it never be! For if a law had been given which was able to impart life, then righteousness would indeed have been based on law. But the Scripture has shut up all men under sin, that the promise by faith in Jesus Christ might be given to those who believe. . . . Therefore the Law has become our tutor to lead us to Christ, that we may be justified by faith" (Gal. 3:6-24). "For by grace you have been saved through faith; and that not of yourselves, it is the gift of God; not as a result of works, that no one should boast. For we are His workmanship, created in Christ Jesus for good works, which God prepared beforehand, that we should walk in them" (Eph. 2:8-10). "There is therefore now no condemnation for those who are in Christ Jesus. For the law of the Spirit of life in Christ Jesus has set you free from the law of sin and of death. For what the Law could not do, weak as it was through the flesh, God did: sending His own Son in the likeness of sinful flesh and as an offering for sin, He condemned sin in the flesh, in order that the requirement of the Law might be fulfilled in us, who do not walk according to the flesh, but according to the Spirit" (Rom. 8:1-4).

f. "He saved us, not on the basis of deeds which we have done in righteousness, but according to His mercy, by the washing of regeneration and renewing by the Holy Spirit" (Tit. 3:5). "[E]ven when we were dead in our transgressions, [God] made us alive together with Christ" (Eph. 2:5). "No one can come to Me, unless the Father who sent Me draws him; and I will raise him up on the last day" (John 6:44). "All that the Father gives Me shall come to Me, and the one who comes to Me I will certainly not cast out" (John 6:37). "You did not choose Me, but I chose you, and appointed you, that you should go and bear fruit. . . ." (John 15:16). "In this is love, not that we loved God, but that He loved us and sent His Son to be the propitiation for our sins. . . . We love, because He first loved us" (1 John 4:10, 19).

Section III: The Biblical System Upheld By Historic Protestant Creeds and Doctrinal Standards

Like Scripture, the historic Protestant creeds and doctrinal standards contradict each and every essential point of Moral Government Theology. They affirm (1) God's absolute and unchangeable foreknowledge, including His perfect foreknowledge of all acts of men and all His own acts; (2) God's absolute and unchangeable goodness; (3) the doctrines of original sin and human moral inability; (4) that the atonement consists in Christ's paying sinners' debt and bearing their punishment for sin as their substitute in satisfaction of the demands of God's justice; and (5) that believers, without any merit or works of their own, are justified by grace through faith in the atoning work of Christ and have the righteousness of Christ imputed to them. In this section we set forth the positions of the main Calvinist, Lutheran, and Wesleyan creeds and (because proponents of Moral Government Theology perversely claim to be Wesleyan Arminians) the writings of James Arminius and John Wesley on these points.

Note: The numbered points below correspond to the numbered points in each of the two preceding sections. The lettered points, however, do not correspond to the lettered points in the preceding sections but delineate the theological sources presented. The lettered points, then, provide general *contrast to* the numbered points in section I and general *agreement with* the numbered points in section II.

1. The Historic Doctrine of God's Foreknowledge

a. Lutheran: "[T]he foreknowledge of God is nothing else than this, that God knows all things before they come to pass. . . . This foreknowledge of God extends both to good and evil men; but nevertheless it is not the cause of evil, nor is it the cause of sin, impelling man to crime."[83]

b. Calvinist: "God, the great Creator of all things, doth uphold, direct, dispose, and govern all creatures, actions, and things, from the greatest even to the least, by his most wise and holy providence, according to his infallible foreknowledge and the free and immutable counsel of his own will, to the praise of the glory of his wisdom, power, justice, goodness, and mercy. . . . Although in relation to the foreknowledge and decree of God, the first cause all things come to pass immutably and infallibly, yet by the same providence he ordereth them to fall out, according to the nature of second causes, either necessarily, freely, or contingently."[84]

c. Wesleyan: "There is but one living and true God, everlasting, without body or parts, of *infinite* power, *wisdom*, and goodness. . . ."[85]

[83] *Formula of Concord*, Article XI, Affirmative, sects. ii-iii.
[84] *Westminster Confession*, Chapter V, Articles i-ii.
[85] *Methodist Articles of Religion*, Article I.

d. Arminius: "IMMUTABILITY is a pre-eminent mode of the Essence of God, by which it is void of all change; of being transferred from place to place, because it is itself its own end and good, and because it is immense; of generation and corruption; of alteration; increase and decrease; for the same reason as that by which it is incapable of suffering. (Psalm cii, 27; Mal. iii, 6; James i, 17.) Whence likewise, in the Scriptures, INCORRUPTIBILITY is attributed to God."[86] "God . . . knows all things possible, whether they be in the capability of God or of the creature; in active or passive capability; in the capability of operation, imagination, or enunciation. He knows all things that could have an existence, on laying down any hypothesis. He knows [*alia a se*] other things than himself, those which are necessary and contingent, good and bad, universal and particular, future, present and past, excellent and vile. He knows things substantial and accidental of every kind; the actions and passions, the modes and circumstances of all things; external words and deeds, internal thoughts, deliberations, counsels, and determinations, and the entities of reason, whether complex or simple. All these things, being jointly attributed to the understanding of God, seem to conduce to the conclusion, that God may deservedly be said to know things infinite. (Acts xv, 18; Heb. iv, 13; Matt. xi, 27; Psalm cxlvii, 4; Isai. xli, 22, 23; xliv, 7; Matt. x, 30; Psalm cxxxv; 1 John iii, 20; 1 Sam. xvi, 7; 1 Kings viii, 39; Psalm xciv, 11; Isai. xl, 28; Psalm cxlvii, 5; cxxxix; xciv, 9, 10; x, 13, 14.) . . . All the things which God knows, He knows neither by intelligible [species] images, nor by similitude, (for it is not necessary for Him to use abstraction and application for the purpose of understanding); but He knows them by his own essence, and by this alone, with the exception of evil things which He knows indirectly by the opposite good things; as, through means of the habitude, privation is discovered. THEREFORE, 1. God knows himself *entirely* and *adequately*

---

[86] Arminius, *Public Disputations*, IV, xviii.

. . . . 2. He knows himself primarily; . . . 3. [*Intelligere Dei*] The act of understanding in God is his own being and essence. . . . The mode by which God understands, is not that which is successive, and which is either through composition or division, or through [*discursum*] deductive argumentation; but it is simple, and through infinite intuition. (Heb. iv, 13.) THEREFORE, 1. God knows all things from eternity; nothing [*de novo*] recently. For this new perfection would add something to His essence by which He understands all things; or his understanding would exceed His essence, if he now understood what he did not formerly understand. But this cannot happen, since he understands all things through his essence. (Acts xv, 18; Ephe. i, 4.) 2. He knows all things immeasurably, without the augmentation and decrease of the things known and of the knowledge itself. (Psalm cxlvii, 5.) 3. He knows all things immutably, his knowledge not being varied to the infinite changes of the things known. (James i, 17.) 4. By a single and [*individuo*] undivided act, not [*distractus*] being diverted towards many things but collected into himself, He knows all things. Yet he does not know them confusedly, or only universally and in general; but also in a distinct and most special manner He knows himself in himself, things in their causes, in themselves, in his own essence, in themselves [*praesenter*] as being present, in their causes antecedently, and in himself most pre-eminently. (Heb. iv, 13; 1 Kings viii, 39; Psalm cxxxix, 16, 17.) . . . The understanding of God is certain, and never can be deceived, so that He certainly and infallibly sees even future contingencies, whether He sees them in their causes or in themselves. (1 Sam. xxiii, 11, 12; Matt. xi, 21.) But, this certainty rests upon the infinite essence of God, by which in a manner the most present He understands all things. . . . The understanding of God [*causatur*] is derived from no external cause, not even from an object; though if there should not afterwards be an object,

[87] *Ibid.*, IV, xxxi-xxxiii, xxxvi-xxxvii.

[*non sit de eo futura*], there would not likewise be the understanding of God about it. (Isai. xl, 13, 14; Rom. xi, 33, 34.)"[87]

e. Wesley, commenting on John 6:64, "For Jesus had known from the beginning who they were that believed not, and who would betray him": "Therefore it is plain, God does foresee future contingencies:—

'But his foreknowledge causes not the fault,
Which had no less proved certain unforeknown.'"[88]

2. The Historic Doctrine of God's Goodness [89]

a. Lutheran: Neither the *Augsburg Confession* nor the *Formula of Concord* explicitly affirms the moral immutability of God. Neither, however, denies it. Luther, however, in lecturing on Romans 1:17, argues that the righteousness of God is distinct from the righteousness of men in that, in men, "righteousness follows upon and flows from actions. But, according to God, righteousness precedes works and works result from it."[90] Thus Luther roots the character of God's works in His internal moral character, not God's moral character in the character of His works.

b. Calvinist: "God is a spirit, infinite, eternal, and *un-*

---

[88] Wesley, *Explanatory Notes*, p. 232.

[89] It might come as something of a surprise that the major creeds take so little trouble to state and defend explicitly the moral immutability of God, but the explanation is simple: Creeds normally develop in antithesis to error; where there is no error, or where error is uncommon, held only in confusion and readily abandoned when corrected, or considered so obviously false as to warrant no explicit opposition, the creeds are likely to say little; where, however, error is common, held tenaciously despite correction, or considered so subtle as easily to deceive even the cautious, the creeds speak fully. In general circles the immutable goodness of God was never questioned. In some circles near Arminius, however, it was questioned and even denied. Hence Arminius goes to great length to defend the doctrine of God's immutable goodness, while the creeds of the churches treat it only briefly and as unchallenged.

[90] Martin Luther, *Lectures on Romans*, trans. Wilhelm Pauck (Philadelphia: Westminster, 1961), p. 18.

changeable, in his being, wisdom, power, holiness, justice, *goodness*, and truth."[91]

c. Wesleyan: "There is but one living and true God, everlasting, without body or parts, of *infinite* power, wisdom, and *goodness*. . . ."[92]

d. Arminius: ". . . [some] brought forward an instance, or example, in which [they alleged that] Necessity and Liberty met together; and that was God, who is both necessarily and freely good. This assertion of theirs displeased me so exceedingly, as to cause me to say, *that it was not far removed from blasphemy*. At this time, I entertain a similar opinion about it; and in a few words I thus prove its *falsity*, *absurdity*, and the *blasphemy* [contained] *in the falsity*. (1.) Its *falsity*. He who by *natural necessity*, and according to his very essence and the whole of his nature, is good, nay, who is Goodness itself, the Supreme Good, the First Good from whom all good proceeds, through whom every good comes, in whom every good exists, and by a participation of whom what things soever have any portion of good in them are good, and more or less good as they are nearer or more remote from it. He is not FREELY good. For it is a contradiction in an adjunct, or an opposition in an apposition. But God is good by natural necessity, according to his entire nature and essence, and is Goodness itself, the supreme and primary Good, from whom, through whom, and in whom is all good, &c. Therefore, **God is not freely good**. (2.) Its *absurdity*. Liberty is an affection of the Divine Will; not of the Divine Essence, Understanding, or Power; and therefore it is not an affection of the Divine Nature, considered in its totality. It is indeed an effect of the will, according to which it is borne towards an object that is neither primary nor adequate, and that is different from God himself; and this effect of the will, therefore, is posterior in order to that affection of the will according to which God is

---

[91] *Westminster Shorter Catechism*, Ques. 4, emphases added.
[92] *Methodist Articles of Religion*, Article I, emphases added.

borne towards a proper, primary and adequate object, which is himself. But Goodness is an affection of the whole of the Divine Nature, Essence, Life, Understanding, Will, Power, &c. Therefore, **God is not freely good**; that is, **he is not good by the mode of liberty, but by that of natural necessity.** . . . (3.) I prove that *blasphemy* is contained in this assertion: because, if God be freely good, (that is, not by nature and natural necessity,) he can be or can be made *not good*. As whatever any one wills freely, he has it in his power *not to will*; and whatever any one does freely, he can refrain from doing. . . . [T]he Christian Fathers justly attached blasphemy to those who said, 'the Father begat the Son *willingly*, or by his own will;' because from this it would follow, that the Son had [*principium*] an origin similar to that of the creatures. But with how much greater equity does blasphemy fasten itself upon those who declare, 'that God is *freely* good!'"[93]

e. United Church of Canada: "We believe in the one only living and true God, a Spirit infinite, eternal, and *unchangeable*, in His being and perfections; the Lord Almighty, who is love, most just in all His ways, most glorious in holiness, unsearchable in wisdom, plenteous in mercy, full of compassion, abundant in goodness and truth."[94]

f. Wesley: "[God] is infinite in wisdom as well as in power: and all his wisdom is continually employed in managing all the affairs of his creation for the good of all his creatures. For his wisdom and goodness go hand in hand: they are inseparably united, and continually act in concert with almighty power, for the real good of all his creatures. . . . And to Him all things are possible. . . . Only He that can do all things else cannot deny Himself: He cannot counteract Himself, or oppose his own work."[95] "[Christ's] divine righteousness belongs

[93] Arminius, *Apology*, Article XXII, italicized emphases original, boldfaced emphases added.

[94] *Basis of Union* of the United Church of Canada, Article I, emphasis added. The UCC is a union of the Presbyterian, Methodist, and Congregational churches in Canada originating in 1910.

[95] *By John Wesley*, pp. 20-21; extracted from the sermon "Divine Providence" in *The Works of the Rev. John Wesley*, 2:99-107.

to his divine nature. . . . Now this is his eternal, essential, *immutable*, holiness; his infinite justice, mercy, and truth: in all which, He and the Father are one."[96]

3. The Historic Doctrine of Original Sin and Inability

a. Lutheran: "[A]fter Adam's fall, all men begotten after the common course of nature are born with sin; that is, without the fear of God, without trust in him, and with fleshly appetite; and that this disease, or original fault, is truly sin, condemning and bringing eternal death now also upon all that are not born again. . . ."[97] "[M]an's will hath some liberty to work a civil righteousness, and to choose such things as reason can reach unto; but . . . hath no power to work the righteousness of God, or a spiritual righteousness, without the Spirit of God; because that the natural man receiveth not the things of the Spirit of God (1 Cor. ii. 14). . . . [The Lutheran Churches] condemn the Pelagians and others, who teach that by the power of nature alone, without the Spirit of God, we are able to love God above all things; also to perform the commandments of God, as touching the substance of our actions. For although nature be able in some sort to do the external works . . . yet it can not work the inward motions, such as the fear of God, trust in God, chastity, patience, and such like."[98] ". . . we believe, teach, and confess that Original Sin is no trivial corruption, but is so profound a corruption of human nature as to leave nothing sound, nothing uncorrupt in the body or soul of man, or in his mental or bodily powers. As reads the hymn of the Church: 'Through Adam's fall is all corrupt, Nature and essence human.' . . . And we indeed affirm that no one is able to dissever this corruption of the nature from the nature itself, except God alone, which will fully come to pass by means of death in the resurrection

---

[96] *Ibid.*, pp. 62-3; extracted from Wesley's sermon "The Lord of Righteousness," in *Standard Sermons of John Wesley*, 2:426-7.

[97] *Augsburg Confession*, Article II.

[98] *Ibid.*, Article XVIII.

unto blessedness. . . . We therefore reject and condemn that dogma by which it is asserted that Original Sin is merely the liability and debt of another's transgression, transmitted to us apart from any corruption of our nature. . . . Also, [we reject and condemn that dogma] that depraved concupiscences are not sin, but certain concreate[99] conditions and essential properties of the nature, or that those defects and that huge evil just set forth by us is not sin on whose account man, if not grafted into Christ, is a child of wrath. . . . We also reject the Pelagian heresy, in which it is asserted that the nature of man after the fall is incorrupt, and that, moreover in spiritual things it has remained wholly good and pure in its natural powers. . . . Also, [we reject and condemn the dogma] that Original Sin is an external impediment of sound spiritual powers, and is not a despoliation and defect thereof. . . . Also, [we reject and condemn the dogma] that man's nature and essence are not utterly corrupt, but that there is something of good still remaining in man, even in spiritual things, to wit, goodness, capacity, aptitude, ability, industry, or the powers by which in spiritual things he has strength to undertake, effect, or co-effect somewhat of good. . . . For Original Sin is not a particular transgression which is perpetrated in act, but intimately inheres, being infixed in the very nature, substance, and essence of man. And, indeed, if no depraved thought at all should ever arise in the heart of fallen man, if no idle word were uttered, if no evil work or deed were perpetrated by him: yet, nevertheless, the nature is corrupted by Original Sin, which is innate in us by reason of the corrupted seed from which we spring, and is, moreover, a fountain of all other actual sins, such as evil thoughts, evil discoursings, evil and abominable deeds. For thus it is written, as we read in Matthew xv. 19: 'For out of the heart proceed evil thoughts.' And elsewhere (Gen. vi. 5; viii. 21): 'Every imagination of

[99] *Concreate*, as in the text, is the correct word. It means "created with."

the thought of man's heart is only evil from his youth.'"[100] ". . . the understanding and reason of man in spiritual things are wholly blind, and can understand nothing by their proper powers. [*cit.* 1 Cor. 2:14.] . . . We believe, teach, and confess, moreover, that the yet unregenerate will of man is not only averse from God, but has become even hostile to God, so that it only wishes and desires those things, and is delighted with them, which are evil and opposite to the divine will. [*cit.* Gen. 8:28; Rom. 8:7.] . . . Therefore we believe that by how much it is impossible that a dead body should vivify itself and restore corporal life to itself, even so impossible is it that man, who by reason of sin is spiritually dead, should have any faculty of recalling himself into spiritual life [*cit.* Eph. 2:5; 2 Cor. 3:5]. . . ."[101] "We repudiate, also, that gross error of the Pelagians, who have not hesitated to assert that man by his own powers, without the grace of the Holy Spirit, has ability to convert himself to God, to believe the gospel, to obey the divine law from his heart, and in this way to merit of himself the remission of sins and eternal life. . . . Besides these errors, we reject also the false dogma of the Semi-Pelagians, who teach that man by his own powers can commence his conversion, but can not fully accomplish it without the grace of the Holy Spirit. . . . Also the teaching that, although unregenerate man, in respect of free-will, is indeed, antecedently to his regeneration, too infirm to make a beginning of his own conversion, and by his own powers to convert himself to God, and obey the law of God with all his heart; yet if the Holy Spirit by the preaching of the word, shall have made a beginning, and offered his grace in the word to man, that then man, by his own proper and natural powers, can, as it were, give some assistance and co-operation, though it be but slight, infirm, and languid, towards his con-

---

[100] *Formula of Concord*, Article I, Affirmative, sect. iii, Negative, sects. i-vi, xi.

[101] *Ibid.*, Article II, Affirmative, sects. i-ii.

version, and can apply and prepare himself unto grace, apprehend it, embrace it, and believe the gospel."[102]

b. Calvinist: "Our first parents, being seduced by the subtilty and temptation of Satan, sinned in eating the forbidden fruit. . . . By this sin they fell from their original righteousness and communion with God, and so became dead in sin, and wholly defiled in all the faculties and parts of soul and body. . . . They being the root of all mankind, the guilt of this sin was imputed, and the same death in sin and corrupted nature conveyed to all their posterity descending from them by ordinary generation. . . . From this original corruption, whereby we are utterly indisposed, disabled, and made opposite to all good, and wholly inclined to all evil, do proceed all actual transgressions. . . . Every sin, both original and actual, being a transgression of the righteous law of God, and contrary thereunto, doth, in its own nature, bring guilt upon the sinner, whereby he is bound over to the wrath of God and curse of the law, and so made subject to death, with all miseries spiritual, temporal, and eternal."[103] "Man, by his fall into a state of sin, hath wholly lost all ability of will to any spiritual good accompanying salvation; so as a natural man, being altogether averse from that good, and dead in sin, is not able, by his own strength, to convert himself, or to prepare himself thereunto. . . . When God converts a sinner, and translates him into the state of grace, he freeth him from his natural bondage under sin, and by his grace alone enables him freely to will and to do that which is spiritually good; yet so as that, by reason of his remaining corruption, he doth not perfectly, nor only, will that which is good, but doth also will that which is evil."[104]

c. Wesleyan: ". . . Christ . . . suffered, was crucified, dead and buried, to reconcile his Father to us, and to be a sacrifice, *not only for original guilt*, but also for the actual sins of men.

[102] *Ibid.*, Article II, Affirmative, sects. i, ii, Negative, sects. ii-iv.

[103] *Westminster Confession*, Chapter VI, Articles i-iv, vi.

[104] *Ibid.*, Chapter IX, Articles iii and iv.

. . . Original sin standeth not in the following of Adam (as the Pelagians do vainly talk), but it is the corruption of the nature of every man, that naturally is engendered of the offspring of Adam, whereby man is very far gone from original righteousness, and of his own nature inclined to evil, and that continually. . . . The condition of man after the fall of Adam is such that he can not turn and prepare himself, by his own natural strength and works, to faith and calling upon God; wherefore we have no power to do good works, pleasant and acceptable to God, without the grace of God by Christ preventing [working first in] us, that we may have a good will, and working with us, when we have that good will."[105]

d. Arminius: "This is my opinion concerning the Free-will of man: *In his primitive condition* as he came out of the hands of his Creator, man was endowed with such a portion of knowledge, holiness and power, as enabled him to understand, esteem, consider, will and to perform THE TRUE GOOD, according to the commandment delivered to him. Yet none of these acts could he do, *except through the assistance of Divine Grace*. But in his *lapsed and sinful state*, man is not capable, of and by himself, either to think, to will, or to do that which is really good; but it is necessary for him to be regenerated and renewed in his intellect, affections or will, and in all his powers, by God in Christ through the Holy Spirit, that he may be qualified rightly to understand, esteem, consider, will, and perform whatever is truly good. When he is made a partaker of this regeneration or renovation, I consider that, since he is delivered from sin, he is capable of thinking, willing and doing that which is good, but yet *not without the continued aids of Divine Grace*."[106] "The proper and immediate effect of [Adam's first] sin was the offending of the Deity. . . . From this violation of his law, God conceives just displeasure, which is the second effect of sin. ([Gen.] iii, 16-

[105] *Methodist Articles of Religion*, Articles II, VII, and VIII.

[106] Arminius, *Declaration of Sentiments*, III.

19, 23, 24.) But to anger succeeds infliction of punishment, which was in this instance two-fold. (1.) [*Reatus*] A liability to two deaths ([Gen.] ii, 17; Rom. vi, 23). (2.) [*Privatio*] The withdrawing of that primitive righteousness and holiness, which, because they are the effects of the Holy Spirit dwelling in man, ought not to have remained in him after he had fallen from the favor of God, and had incurred the Divine displeasure (Luke xix, 26). For this Spirit is a seal of God's favor and good will (Rom. viii, 14, 15; 1 Cor. ii, 12). . . . The whole of this sin, however, is not peculiar to our first parents, but is common to the entire race and to all their posterity, who, at the time when this sin was committed, were in their loins, and who have since descended from them by the natural mode of propagation, according to the primitive benediction. For in Adam 'all have sinned.' (Rom. v, 12.) Wherefore, whatever punishment was brought down upon our first parents, has likewise pervaded and yet pursues all their posterity. So that all men 'are by nature the children of wrath,' (Ephes. ii, 3,) obnoxious to condemnation, and to temporal as well as to eternal death; they are also devoid of that original righteousness and holiness. (Rom. vi, 12, 18, 19.) With these evils they would remain oppressed forever, unless they were liberated by Christ Jesus; to whom be glory forever."[107]

"In the state of PRIMITIVE INNOCENCE, man had a mind endued with a clear understanding of heavenly light and truth concerning God, and his works and will, as far as was sufficient for the salvation of man and the glory of God; he had a heart imbued with 'righteousness and true holiness,' and with a true and saving love of good; and powers abundantly [*instructas*] qualified or furnished perfectly to fulfill the law which God had imposed on him. . . . But man was not so confirmed in this state of innocence, as to be incapable of being moved, [*specie*] by the representation presented to him of some good, (whether it was of an inferior kind and relat-

[107] Arminius, *Public Disputations*, VII, xv-xvi.

ing to this animal life, or of a superior kind and relating to spiritual life,) inordinately and unlawfully to look upon it and to desire it, and of his own spontaneous as well as free motion, and through a preposterous desire for that good, to decline from the obedience which had been prescribed to him. Nay, [*aversus*] having turned away from the light of his own mind and his chief good, which is God, or, at least [*conversus*] having turned towards that chief good not in the manner in which he ought to have done, and besides having turned in mind and heart towards an inferior good, he transgressed the command given to him for life. By this foul deed, he precipitated himself from that noble and elevated condition into a state of the deepest infelicity, which is UNDER THE DOMINION OF SIN. . . . In this state, the free will of man towards the true good is not only wounded, maimed, infirm, bent, and [*attenuatum*] weakened; but it is also [*captivatum*] imprisoned, destroyed, and lost. And its powers are not only debilitated and useless unless they be assisted by grace, but it has no powers whatever except such as are excited by Divine grace. For Christ has said, 'Without me ye can do nothing.' . . . 1. *The mind* of man, in this state, is dark, destitute of the saving knowledge of God, and according to the Apostle, incapable of those things which belong to the Spirit of God. . . . 2. To the darkness of the mind succeeds *the perverseness of the affections and of the heart*, according to which it hates and has an aversion to that which is truly good and pleasing to God; but it loves and pursues what is evil. The Apostle was unable to afford a more luminous description of this perverseness, than he has given in the following words: 'The carnal mind is enmity against God. For it is not subject to the law of God, neither indeed can be. So then, they that are in the flesh cannot please God.' (Rom. viii, 7.) . . . 3. Exactly correspondent to this darkness of the mind, and perverseness of the heart, is [*impotentia*] the utter weakness of all the powers to perform that which is truly good, and to omit the perpetration of that which is evil, in a due mode and from a due end and cause. The subjoined sayings of Christ serve to describe this impotence. 'A corrupt tree cannot bring forth good fruit.' (Matt. vii, 18.) 'How can ye, being evil, speak good things?' (xii, 34.) The following relates to the good which is properly described in the gospel: 'No man can come to me, except the Father draw him.' (John vi, 44.) As do likewise the following words of the Apostle: 'The carnal mind is not subject to the law of God, neither indeed can be;' (Rom. vii, 7;) therefore, that man over whom it has dominion, *cannot perform what the law commands. . . .*"[108]

e. Wesley: "The state of a natural man the Scripture represents as a state of sleep: the voice of God to him is, 'Awake, thou that sleepest.' For his soul is in a deep sleep: his spiritual senses are not awake: they discern neither spiritual good nor evil. The eyes of his understanding are closed; they are sealed together, and see not. Clouds and darkness continually rest upon them; for he lies in the valley of the shadow of death. Hence, having no inlets for the knowledge of spiritual things, all the avenues of his soul being shut up, he is in gross, stupid ignorance of whatever he is most concerned to know. He is utterly ignorant of God, knowing nothing concerning him as he ought to know. He is totally a stranger to the law of God, as to its true, inward, spiritual meaning. He has no conception of that evangelical holiness, without which no man shall see the Lord; nor of the happiness which they only find whose 'life is hid with Christ in God.'

"And, for this very reason, because he is fast asleep, he is, in some sense, at rest. Because he is blind, he is also secure: he saith, 'Tush, there shall no harm happen unto me.' The darkness which covers him on every side, keeps him in a kind of peace; so far as peace can consist with works of the devil, and with an earthly, devilish mind. He sees not that he stands on the edge of the pit; therefore he fears it not. He cannot tremble at the danger he does not know. He has not understanding enough to fear.

---

[108] *Ibid.*, VIII, v.

"Why is it that he is in no dread of God? Because he is totally ignorant of Him: if not saying in his heart, 'There is no God'; or, that 'He sitteth on the circle of the heavens, and humbleth' yet satisfying himself as well, to all Epicurean intents and purposes, by saying, 'God is merciful'; confounding and swallowing up at once in that unwieldy idea of mercy all his holiness and essential hatred of sin; all his justice, wisdom and truth. He is in no dread of the vengeance denounced against those who obey not the blessed law of God, because he understands it not. He imagines the main point is, to do thus, to be outwardly blameless; and sees not that it extends to every temper, desire, thought, motion of the heart. Or he fancies that the obligation hereto is ceased; that Christ came to 'destroy the Law and the Prophets'; to save his people in, not from, their sins; to bring them to heaven without holiness—notwithstanding his own words, 'Not one jot or tittle of the law shall pass away, till all things are fulfilled'; and, 'Not every one that saith unto me, Lord, Lord! shall enter into the kingdom of heaven; but he that doeth the will of my Father which is in heaven.'

"He is secure, because he is utterly ignorant of himself. Hence he talks of 'repenting by-and-by'; he does not indeed exactly know when, but some time or other before he dies; taking it for granted, that this is quite in his own power. For what should hinder his doing it, if he will? If he does but once set a resolution, no fear but he will make it good!

"But this ignorance never so strongly glares, as in those who are termed men of learning. If a natural man be one of these, he can talk at large of his rational faculties, of the freedom of his will, and the absolute necessity of such freedom, in order to constitute man a moral agent. He reads, and argues, and proves to a demonstration, that every man may do as he will; may dispose his own heart to evil or good, as it seems best in his own eyes. Thus the god of this world spreads a double veil of blindness over his heart, lest, by any means, 'the light of the glorious gospel of Christ should shine' upon it.

"From the same ignorance of himself and God, there may sometime arise, in the natural man, a kind of joy, in congratulating himself upon his own wisdom and goodness; and what the world calls joy he may often possess. He may have pleasure in various kinds; either in gratifying the desires of the flesh, or the desire of the eye, or the pride of life; particularly if he has large possessions; if he enjoys an affluent fortune; then he may 'clothe himself in purple and fine linen and fare sumptuously every day.' And so long as he thus doeth well unto himself, men will doubtless speak good of him. They will say, 'He is a happy man.' For, indeed, this is the sum of worldly happiness; to dress, and visit, and talk, and eat, and drink, and rise up to play.

"It is not surprising, if one in such circumstances as these, dosed with the opiates of flattery and sin, should imagine, among his other waking dreams, that he walks in great liberty. How easily may he persuade himself, that he is at liberty from all vulgar errors, and from the prejudice of education; judging exactly right, and keeping clear of all extremes. 'I am free,' may he say, 'from all the enthusiasm of weak and narrow souls; from superstition, the disease of fools and cowards, always righteous over much; and from bigotry, continually incident to those who have not a free and generous way of thinking.' And too sure it is that he is altogether free from the 'wisdom which cometh from above,' from holiness, from the religion of the heart, from the whole mind which was in Christ.

"For all this time he is the servant of sin. He commits sin, more or less, day by day. Yet he is not troubled: he 'is in no bondage,' as some speak; he feels no condemnation. He contents himself (even though he should profess to believe that the Christian revelation is of God) with 'Man is frail. We are all weak. Every man has his infirmity.' Perhaps he quotes Scripture: 'Why does not Solomon say, The righteous man falls into sin seven times a day? And, doubtless they are all hypocrites or enthusiasts who pretend to be better than their neighbors.' If, at any time, a serious thought fix upon him, he stifles it as soon as possible, with 'Why should I fear, since God is merciful, and Christ died for sinners?'

"Thus, he remains *a willing servant of sin, content with the bondage of corruption; inwardly and outwardly unholy, and satisfied therewith; not only not conquering sin, but not striving to conquer*, particularly that sin which doth so easily beset him."[109]

"This, therefore, is the first grand distinguishing point between Heathenism and Christianity. The one acknowledges that many men are infected with many vices, and even born with a proneness to them; but supposes withal, that in some the natural good much overbalances the evil: the other declares that all men are 'conceived in sin,' and 'shapen in wickedness'—that hence there is in every man a 'carnal mind', which is enmity against God; which is not, cannot be, subject to 'his law'; which so infects the whole soul, that 'there dwelleth in' him 'in his flesh,' in his natural state, 'no good thing'; but 'every imagination of the thoughts of his heart is evil,' only evil, and that 'continually.'

"Hence we may learn that all who deny this, call it 'original sin,' or by any other title, are but Heathens still, in the fundamental point which differences Heathenism from Christianity. They may, indeed, allow, that men have many vices; that some are born with us; and that, consequently, we are not born altogether so wise or so virtuous as we should be; there being few that will roundly affirm, 'We are born with as much propensity to good as to evil, and that every man is, by nature as virtuous and wise as Adam was at creation.' But here is the shibboleth: Is man by nature filled with all manner of evil? Is he void of all good? Is he wholly fallen? Is his soul totally corrupted? Or, to come back to the text, is 'every

---

[109] *By John Wesley*, pp. 24-29; extracted from Wesley's sermon, "The Spirit of Bondage and of Adoption," in *Standard Sermons of John Wesley*, 1:181-5.

imagination of the thoughts of his heart only evil continually?'

"Allow this, and you are so far a Christian. Deny it, and you are but a Heathen still."[110]

"Now God saw that all this, the whole thereof, was evil;—contrary to moral rectitude; contrary to the nature of God, which necessarily includes all good;[111] contrary to the divine will, the eternal standard of good and evil; contrary to the pure, holy image of God, wherein man was originally created, and wherein he stood when God, surveying the works of his hands, saw them all to be very good; contrary to justice, mercy, and truth, and to the essential relations which each man bore to his Creator and his fellow-creatures.

"But was there not good mingled with the evil? Was there not light intermixed with the darkness? No; none at all: 'God saw that the whole imagination of the heart of man was only evil.' It cannot indeed be denied, but many of them, perhaps all, had good motions put into their hearts; for the Spirit of God did then also 'strive with man,' if haply he might repent, more especially during the gracious reprieve, the hundred and twenty years, while the ark was preparing. But still 'in his flesh dwelt no good thing;' *all his nature was purely evil* (emphasis added): It was wholly consistent with itself, and unmixed with anything of an opposite nature.

"However, it may still be a matter of inquiry, 'Was there no intermission of this evil? Were there no lucid intervals, wherein something good might be found in the heart of man?' We are not here to consider, what the grace of God might occasionally work in his soul; and, abstracted from this, we have no reason to believe, there was any intermission of that evil. For God, who 'saw the whole imagination of the thoughts of his heart to be *only* (emphasis original) evil,' saw likewise,

---

[110] *Ibid.*, pp. 29-30; extracted from Wesley's sermon "Original Sin" in *Standard Sermons of John Wesley*, 2:222-5.

[111] Note that Wesley here locates God's goodness not in His volition but in His nature, and says that that nature *necessarily* includes all good.

that it was always the same, that it 'was only evil *continually* (emphasis original);' every year, every day, every hour, every moment. He never deviated into good."[112]

4. The Historic Doctrine of the Atonement

a. Lutheran: "[T]he Word . . . truly suffered, was crucified, dead, and buried, that he might reconcile the Father unto us, and might be a sacrifice, not only for original guilt, but also for all actual sins of men."[113]

b. Calvinist: "The Lord Jesus, by his perfect obedience and sacrifice of himself, which he through the eternal Spirit once offered up unto God, hath fully satisfied the justice of his Father, and purchased not only reconciliation, but an everlasting inheritance in the kingdom of heaven, for all those

---

[112] John Wesley, "Original Sin," in *The Works of John Wesley*, 14 vols. (1872; reprint ed., Grand Rapids: Zondervan, 1958-59), 6:56-57. Cited in Paul A. Mickey, *Essentials of Wesleyan Theology: A Contemporary Affirmation* (Grand Rapids, MI: Zondervan, 1980), p. 82. Mickey further explains the Wesleyan doctrine of original sin:

"Adam and Eve were the prototype of humanity, and their action has been *determinative* for each person since. Through disobedience they corrupted the close and intimate relationship they had enjoyed with God. This corruption is pervasive and permeates all of human life. Wesley viewed sin as pervasive ("*only* evil") and persistent ("was only evil *continually*"). Sin extends to all that is touched by the human spirit. . . ." (pp. 82-3)

"The pervasive corruption of original sin is (1) a sin bequeathed (sin inherited and transmitted by and through humanity) and (2) a sin begotten (sin initiated and created by and through human activities). Sin presents itself in two guises: that which is endowed and that which is initiated. This dual character of original sin prevents men and women from making a positive response to God's offer of redemption and fellowship. . . . We cannot turn from sin on our own. The sinner is convicted and wooed first by the Holy Spirit. The depths of sin, of our turning away from God, are so encompassing of the human spirit that we are utterly cut off from any effective possibility of turning toward God. We cannot offer repentance and receive forgiveness apart from the thoroughgoing work of the Holy Spirit. The abiding presence of original sin so permeates every fiber of human motivation and intentionality that nothing within the human heart would otherwise turn us toward God in repentance" (pp. 84-5).

[113] *Augsburg Confession*, Article III.

whom the Father hath given unto him."[114] "Christ, by his obedience and death, did fully discharge the debt of all those that are thus justified, and did make a proper, real, and full satisfaction to his Father's justice in their behalf. Yet inasmuch as he was given by the Father for them, and his obedience and satisfaction accepted in their stead, and both freely, not for any thing in them, their justification is only of free grace; that both the exact justice and rich grace of God might be glorified in the justification of sinners."[115]

c. Wesleyan: "The Son . . . truly suffered, was crucified, dead and buried, to reconcile his Father to us, and to be a sacrifice, not only for original guilt, but also for the actual sins of men."[116]

d. Arminius: "Nor is it at all repugnant to the merits and satisfaction of Christ, which belong to him as a priest and a victim, that God is himself said to have 'loved the world and given his only begotten Son,' (John iii, 16,) to have delivered him unto death, (Rom. iv, 25,) to have reconciled the world unto himself in Christ, (2 Cor. v, 19,) to have redeemed us, (Luke i, 68,) and to have freely forgiven us our sins. (Rom. iii, 25.) For we must consider the affection of love to be two-fold in God. *The first* is a love for the creature—*The other*, a love for justice, united to which is a hatred against sin. It was the will of God that each of these kinds of love should be satisfied. He gave satisfaction to his *love for the creature* who was a sinner, when he gave up his Son who might act the part of Mediator. But he rendered **satisfaction** to *his love for justice and to his hatred against sin*, when he imposed on his Son the office of Mediator by the shedding of his blood and by the suffering of death; (Heb. ii, 10; v, 8, 9;) and he was unwilling to admit him as the Intercessor for sinners except when sprinkled with his own blood, in which he might be made [*expiatio*] the **propitiation** for sins. (ix, 12.) . . . In this respect

---

[114] *Westminster Confession*, Chapter VIII, Article v.

[115] *Ibid.*, Chapter XI, Article iii.

[116] *Methodist Articles of Religion*, Article II.

also it may with propriety be said that God rendered satisfaction to himself, and appeased himself in 'the Son of his love.'"[117]

e. Wesley:[118] Commenting on 1 John 2:2, which says that Christ is "the propitiation for our sins," Wesley explains *pro-*

---

[117] Arminius, *Public Disputations*, XIV, xvi, italicized emphases original, boldfaced emphases added.

[118] Paul A. Mickey, after quoting John Calvin on the substitutionary satisfaction that Christ, by His death, provided to God's just wrath against sin, added, "Calvin's language supports what is known as the satisfaction theory of the atonement, also held by John and Charles Wesley." *Essentials of Wesleyan Theology*, p. 60. Elsewhere Mickey explains, "In Jesus' sacrificial death God both gives a sacrifice and receives a sacrifice, suffers and is satisfied, and thereby redeems. . . . The 'sinless Son'—to borrow a phrase from John Calvin—has set aside, or appeased, God's holy wrath and righteous anger because of human sin. [paragraph] The doctrine of propitiation (appeasement) of God may be unacceptable to some who prefer to avoid a theological affirmation of God's wrath and anger. To avert one's face from this scriptural truth is to hide in the enormity and pervasiveness of sin and to refuse to face the theological reality of sin" (pp. 128-9). Writing specifically of God's wrath against sin, Mickey adds:

"God's wrath is a holy and righteous anger. It is brought about by our willful violation of God's purpose in creation, not by a distempered spirit in God. Christ did not come nor die to appease the ill temper of a tribal, vindictive god. The wrath and anger affirmed in Scriptures are not the raw emotions of a primitive, bestial god (Gen. 6:6; Exod. 20:5; Lev. 20:23; Deut. 29:20). Our sinful vanity causes us to mislocate the theological truth of God's wrath and anger. But God's righteous anger is not evoked by any emotional instability in Him. It is aroused by the disobedience of a fallen and falling world.

"Traditional Wesleyan theology affirms that the person of God has been offended and violated, not by sociological snubs, but by sin—the human predisposition to replace God without ourselves as the ruler of the universe. Outward and inward violations and offenses exist. God's righteous anger and holy wrath are proper responses to what we have done." (p. 129)

Mickey's book is an excellent summary of Wesleyan theology. No one who has studied it can possibly continue to believe that Moral Government Theology is consistent with authentic Wesleyan theology, whether early or modern. Of it Charles W. Keysor, founder of the Good News renewal movement within United Methodism, wrote, ". . . the emphasis on Wesleyan uniqueness has unfortunately obscured a surprisingly large

pitiation to mean "[t]he atoning sacrifice, by which the wrath of God is appeased."[119] Commenting on Romans 3:25, Wesley writes: ". . . *a propitiation*—To appease an offended God. But if, as some teach, God never was offended, there was no need of this propitiation. And if so, Christ died in vain. *To declare his righteousness*—To demonstrate not only his clemency, but his justice: even that vindictive justice, whose essential character and principal office is, to punish sin. . . ."[120]

5. The Historic Doctrine of Justification

a. Lutheran: "[M]en can not be justified [obtain forgiveness of sins and righteousness] before God by their own powers, merits, or works; but are justified freely [of grace] for Christ's sake through faith, when they believe that they are received into favor, and their sins forgiven for Christ's sake, who by his death hath satisfied for our sins. This faith doth God impute for righteousness before him. Rom. iii. and iv."[121] "[W]e unanimously believe, teach, and confess that Christ is truly our righteousness, but yet neither according to the divine nature alone, nor according to the human nature alone, but the whole Christ according to both natures, to wit: in his sole, most absolute obedience which he rendered to the Father even unto death, as God and man, and thereby merited for us the remission of all our sins and eternal life. As it is written: 'As by one man's disobedience many were made sinners, so by the obedience of one shall many be made righ-

---

common ground that Wesley shared with the magisterial reformers. It is, therefore, both helpful and interesting that Dr. Mickey has chosen to stress the ecumenical commonality that links the thought of Wesley and Calvin. . . . Indeed, the overlapping of Wesleyan, Calvinistic, and Lutheran traditions may be of greater long-range significance than their well-publicized differences. I believe that Dr. Mickey's book contributes significantly to our understanding of what it means to be truly catholic, apostolic, and reformed in faith and doctrine."

[119] Wesley, *Explanatory Notes*, p. 631.

[120] *Ibid.*, p. 370.

[121] *Augsburg Confession*, Article IV.

teous' (Rom. v. 19). . . . We believe, therefore, teach, and confess that this very thing is our righteousness before God, namely, that God remits to us our sins of mere grace, without any respect of our works, going before, present, or following, or of our worthiness or merit. For he bestows and imputes to us the righteousness of the obedience of Christ; for the sake of that righteousness we are received by God into favor and accounted righteous. . . . We believe, also, teach, and confess that Faith alone is the means and instrument whereby we lay hold on Christ the Saviour, and so in Christ lay hold on that righteousness which is able to stand before the judgment of God; for that faith, for Christ's sake, is imputed to us for righteousness (Rom. iv. 5). . . . We believe, teach, and confess, moreover, that, although they that truly believe in Christ and are born again are even to the hour of death obnoxious to many infirmities and stains, yet they ought not to doubt either of the righteousness which is imputed to them through faith or concerning their eternal salvation, but rather are they firmly to be convinced that, for Christ's sake, according to the promise and unshaken word of the gospel, they have God reconciled to them. . . . We repudiate, therefore, and condemn all the false dogmas, which we will now recount: . . . That believers in Christ are righteous and saved before God, both through the imputed righteousness of Christ and through the new obedience which is begun in them. . . . That faith does not justify without good works, that therefore good works are necessarily required for righteousness, and that independently of their being present man can not be justified."[122]

b. Calvinist: "Those whom God effectually calleth he also freely justifieth; not by infusing righteousness into them, but by pardoning their sins, and by accounting and accepting their persons as righteous: not for any thing wrought in them, or

[122] *Formula of Concord*, Article III, Affirmative, sects. i-iii, vi, Negative, sects. ix, xi.

done by them, but for Christ's sake alone; nor by imputing faith itself, the act of believing, or any other evangelical obedience to them, as their righteousness; but by imputing the obedience and satisfaction of Christ unto them, they receiving and resting on him and his righteousness by faith; which faith they have not of themselves, it is the gift of God. . . . Faith, thus receiving and resting on Christ and his righteousness, is the alone instrument of justification; yet is it not alone in the person justified, but is ever accompanied with all other saving graces, and is no dead faith, but worketh by love."[123]

c. Wesleyan: "We are accounted righteous before God only for the merit of our Lord and Saviour Jesus Christ by faith, and not for our own works or deservings. Wherefore, that we are justified by faith only is a most wholesome doctrine, and very full of comfort."[124]

d. Arminius: "I believe that sinners are accounted righteous solely by the obedience of Christ; and that the righteousness of Christ is the only meritorious cause on account of which God pardons the sins of believers and reckons them as righteous as if they had perfectly fulfilled the law. But since God imputes the righteousness of Christ to none except believers, I conclude that, in this sense, it may be well and properly said, *To a man who believes, Faith is imputed for righteousness through grace*, because God hath set forth his Son, Jesus Christ, to be a propitiation, a throne of grace, [or mercy seat] through faith in his blood."[125]

e. Wesley: ". . . as the sin of Adam, without the sins which we afterward committed, brought us death; so the righteousness of Christ, without the good works which we afterward performed, brings us life. . . ."[126] "*As by the disobedience of one man, many*, that is, all men, *were constituted sinners*—Being then in the loins of their first parent, the common head and

[123] *Westminster Confession*, Chapter XI, Articles i and ii.

[124] *Methodist Articles of Religion*, Article IX.

[125] Arminius, *Declaration of Sentiments*, IX.

[126] Wesley, *Explanatory Notes*, p. 375, commenting on Romans 5:14.

representative of them all; *so by the obedience of one*—By his obedience unto death: by his dying for us; *many*—All that believe, *shall be constituted righteous*—Justified, pardoned."[127]

Conclusion

Moral Government Theology, as defined and documented in Section I above, is both *heretical*, in that it is divisive and divided from Christ's true doctrine revealed in Scripture and embraced by the whole Church through the ages, and *blasphemous*, in that it attacks the perfect and unchangeable holiness, goodness, and justice of God and the atoning work of Christ on the Cross. It is not an aberrant form of Christianity but non-Christianity, or, as Wesley described the denial of original sin, "heathenism." It simultaneously debases God by denying His infinite intellectual and moral perfections and exalts man by denying the moral corruption of his nature and asserting instead his moral ability. It is not the real gospel but a false gospel that denies that the substitutionary death of Christ purchases redemption for all who believe, thus denigrating the infinite and perfect value of Christ's propitiatory sacrifice on the Cross and making every man the ultimate cause of his own salvation.

Proponents of Moral Government Theology accuse those who dare to hold their beliefs up to the bright light of Scripture of being divisive. They plea for the unity of the Body of Christ, despite differences in belief. But the real unity of the Body of Christ has nothing to fear from the most diligent testing of doctrine; rather, it is strengthened whenever false doctrine, especially false doctrine that strikes at the defining roots of the faith, is revealed for what it is. Not the defense of orthodoxy, but the propagation and condoning of heresy undermine the unity of the Church.

---

[127] *Ibid.*, p. 376, commenting on Romans 5:19.

Moral Government Theology is one of those winds of doctrine that threaten the growth of the Body of Christ in unity. Against such Paul warned us to be

> no longer . . . children, tossed here and there by the trickery of men, by craftiness in deceitful scheming; but speaking the truth in love, we are to grow up in all aspects into Him, who is the head, even Christ, from whom the whole body, being fitted and held together by that which every joint supplies, according to the proper working of each individual part, causes the growth of the body for the building up of itself in love (Ephesians 4:14-16).

Two attitudes toward Moral Government Theology, in addition to that of actually embracing it, are especially pernicious: (1) Permitting it to be taught as an optional view within Christianity, while professing adherence to the biblical, historic, orthodox view defined and proved above as utterly contradictory to it. This is pernicious because it evidences a lack of (a) appreciation for the perfections of God, (b) repugnance toward the sinfulness of man, and (c) gratitude and awe in regard to the glorious grace of God displayed in the atonement and in justification, and also because it creates confusion among the saints by leading them to believe that one can simultaneously embrace the essential truths of the faith and yet compromise and make way for a system that denies and denigrates them. (2) Pretending that it is merely a form of Arminianism or Wesleyanism. This is pernicious because it both misunderstands and misrepresents the historic doctrines of those two traditions and therefore deceives many unlearned people who are unprepared and ill-equipped to discover the facts, leading them to conceive of Moral Government Theology as consistent with biblical, historic, orthodox Christianity, when in fact it is radically opposed to the faith once for all delivered to the saints. It is particularly regretful that those who claim that Moral Government Theology is consistent with Wesleyanism and Arminianism do so in either ignorance or contempt of the facts about the historic doctrines of those systems.

Some might think us narrow, intolerant, or bigoted for defining Moral Government Theology as outside the bounds of real Christianity. Yet it was John Wesley, who of all great evangelical preachers and theologians was noted highly for his longing for unity among the brethren and peace throughout the Body of Christ, and whose sermon "On the Catholic Spirit" rightly earned him the reputation of one who believed in reaching across doctrinal boundaries to join hands with brothers and sisters, who wrote of the doctrine of original sin, "Allow this, and you are so far a Christian. Deny it, and you are but a Heathen still."[128] If Wesley could make that single doctrine the "shibboleth," as he called it, that distinguished Christian from heathen, how are we to be accused of intolerance if we insist that these five doctrines that all Christian communions have always recognized to be of paramount importance, including that one, are, taken together, defining marks of real Christianity?

We therefore call upon all who call themselves Christians to condemn Moral Government Theology. Not only should it not be embraced among the people of God, but also it should be rejected and fought by them. It is not one among many slight variations on the gospel; it is anti-gospel. It is not one among many varieties of Christianity, it is anti-Christianity. Therefore, all institutions within the Church of God are duty bound to prohibit the teaching and propagating of Moral Government Theology by refusing to permit anyone to teach it under their auspices. Furthermore, any institution that heretofore has permitted the teaching of Moral Government Theology ought, from fidelity to Christ and His Word and from a care for the health of the Body of Christ, to repent publicly of it and to do all in its power to restore those

---

[128] *By John Wesley*, pp. 29-30; extracted from Wesley's sermon "Original Sin" in *Standard Sermons of John Wesley*, 2:222-5.

previously influenced by Moral Government Theology under their auspices to a biblical understanding of the glorious perfections of God, the sinfulness of man, the atoning work of Christ, and justification by grace through faith.

At the same time that we condemn Moral Government Theology as heresy and call on those who have embraced it to turn from it, we rejoice and invite our brothers and sisters to rejoice with us in the beautiful, holy, and miraculous unity of the faith among the chief branches of Protestantism: Lutheran, Calvinist, Arminian, and Wesleyan. The differences that distinguish these traditions, while they are many and real, are dwarfed—as we have seen above—by the solid core of agreement that expresses the unity they have been given in Christ Jesus, the one Son of the one God, revealed by the one Holy Spirit to the one Bride in the one faith. We regret the divisions among us, but we glory in the reality that there is "one body and one Spirit, . . . one hope of [our] calling; one Lord, one faith, one baptism, one God and Father of all who is over all and through all and in all" (Eph. 4:4-6), ever mindful that the Body of Christ is being built up "until we all attain to the unity of the faith, and of the knowledge of the Son of God, to a mature man, to the measure of the stature which belongs to the fullness of Christ" (Eph. 4:13).

About the Author

E. Calvin Beisner is associate professor of interdisciplinary studies at Covenant College, Lookout Mountain, Georgia, and a ruling elder in the Presbyterian Church in America. He writes and speaks often on the application of Christian worldview, theology, and ethics to economics, government, and the environment, and on theological and philosophical apologetics. Calvin and his wife Deborah and their seven children live in a century-old house in the historic St. Elmo district of Chattanooga, Tennessee.

Also By the Author

"Jesus Only" Churches. Grand Rapids: Zondervan, 1996 (forthcoming).

Man, Economy, and the Environment in Biblical Perspective. Moscow, ID: Canon Press, 1994.

Psalms of Promise: Celebrating the Majesty and Faithfulness of God, 2d rev. ed. Phillipsburg, NJ: Presbyterian & Reformed, 1994).

Answers: For Atheists, Agnostics, and Other Thoughtful Skeptics—Dialogs About Christian Faith and Life, rev. ed. Wheaton, IL: Crossway Books, 1993.

Prospects for Growth: A Biblical View of Population, Resources, and the Future. Westchester (now in Wheaton), IL: Crossway Books, 1990, o.p., available from the author.

Prosperity and Poverty: The Compassionate Use of Resources in a World of Scarcity. Westchester (now in Wheaton), IL: Crossway Books, 1988.

God in Three Persons. Wheaton, IL: Tyndale House, 1984, o.p., available from the author